FACE TO FACE WITH YOUR FATHER

A DEVOTIONAL JOURNEY
THROUGH THE GOSPEL OF JOHN

DORRANCE
PUBLISHING CO
EST. 1920
PITTSBURGH, PENNSYLVANIA 15238

Dorrance Publishing Co
585 Alpha Drive
Pittsburgh, PA 15238
Visit our website at *www.dorrancebookstore.com*

ISBN: 978-1-6853-7247-7
eISBN: 978-1-6853-7786-1

*"This devotional study is dedicated to my sisters.
My dears, you are so deeply loved by our Father.
He will never disappoint us. To know Him is to trust Him!
I love you!"*

INTRODUCTION

As far back into childhood as I can remember, I always felt a void in my heart. It was a void I didn't understand and couldn't articulate. Experiences of abuse as a child marred my perception of God until I was convinced He was angry, irritable, judgmental, and abusive. I turned to everything I could that I thought might make me happy and fill that void: anorexia and bulimia, alcohol, self-harm, relationships, even other religions. All the while, I was getting more deeply depressed, and my hopelessness eventually landed me in a psychiatric hospital. A short time later, I was kicked out of my high school and found myself suddenly with a lot more time on my hands. God had been preparing me for that season, and I started reading my Bible every day and turning to Him in crisis. That started a relationship with Him that has blossomed over the last twenty years.

Then, during the summer of 2019, I embarked on a journey I had not anticipated. I joined a workshop at my church because that's what was being offered at the time. Little did I know God my Father had big plans for me. You see, for a long time I have been comfortable praying to Jesus and the Holy Spirit. I spend time with Jesus every morning, and I hear clear direction from the Holy Spirit, but that first person of the Trinity, God the Father, has always made me uncomfortable. Somehow, I decided I wouldn't have to face my "father wounds" because God the Father was for Old Testament believers, and Jesus and the Holy Spirit are for New Testament believers like myself. Obviously, that couldn't be further from the truth.

I let Jesus take my hand that summer and lead me right to my Father. I was scared. I had nightmares. However, every day I sat down with my Bible to open my heart and listen for my Father to speak to me. I have had traumatic experiences with earthly fathers in my lifetime, so getting to know God as my Father was a pretty scary ride.

Scary, but exhilarating. Our Father is so gentle and kind and under-standing. The Holy Spirit spoke so much truth to me that I had to write it all down to remember it! That's where this devotional is coming from.

I read the gospel of John, one verse at a time, and wrote down what I learned about my Father from the words and actions of Jesus. In John 10:30, Jesus said, "I and the Father are One." Again, in John 12:45, Jesus said, "He who sees Me sees the One who sent Me" (see also John 14:7 and Colossians 1:15). The writer of Hebrews said it this way: "The Son is the radiance of His glory and the *exact representation of His nature…*" (Hebrews 1:3, italics mine). Everything I love about Jesus and the Holy Spirit came from the Father – my Father. Somehow, I missed this! Getting to know the Father has been my most worthy task, my highest calling.

Every devotion in this book ends with suggestions for further reading. Look at these verses in context. Sometimes they include God's words to Israel or to a prophet and are not necessarily directed towards you and me. However, *all* of His words teach us His character. We learn how the Father interacts with us when we study His interactions with the people He used to spread His love to the whole world. Every time you sit down to read, ask the Holy Spirit what part of your Father's character He wants you to see.

One more note before we commence: God will never force you to be His child here on earth or in eternity. God is so holy that He cannot allow anyone stained with sin into His perfect home, Heaven. We have all sinned, messed up, literally "missed the mark." Since God is also just, He cannot leave sin unpunished. Your Father loves you so much that He couldn't bear the thought of eternity without you, so He sent Jesus to pay the penalty for your sins. Jesus took your sins to the cross and died for them so you can stand before your Father blameless and ready to spend eternity with Him – if you accept Jesus' sacrifice as payment for your sins. Have you made the decision to get right with the Father? If you haven't, confess your sins to Him and thank Him for sending Jesus to make a way for you to spend eternity with Him.

Knowing my Father and relating to Him as His precious daughter has changed my whole world. When I try to talk to people about God the Father, they often give me a blank stare like I'm crazy, because He's not like any father they know. The purpose of this devotional is so people can get to know their Father as I have gotten to know Him. I pray the Holy Spirit will open your eyes, dear Reader, so you can trust Him and experience His incredible, unending, amazing love. Grab your Bible, and let's get started!

TABLE OF CONTENTS

Your Father hides nothing in the dark. He is Light!

Read John 1:1-9

My childhood was shrouded in secrecy. I was so ashamed of what was done to me that I hid my story from everyone. I saw evil behind the masks of the people who hurt me and my family. I knew the parts they hid from the rest of the world. As most children do, I assumed God was like the authority figures in my life. I expected Him to remove His "Good God" disguise at any moment and reveal His true self. So I kept Him at a distance.

I love that John begins his gospel by introducing Jesus as *the Word* and as *Light*. The Word was a common term used to refer to God Himself. John was making sure we understand that Jesus is "the exact representation" of God the Father (see Hebrews 1:3). Furthermore, the word "Light" gives us the mental image of illumination that allows us to see what is really there. Our Father doesn't need to keep secrets. He doesn't want to hide any part of Himself from us. No matter what our experiences with people have caused us to believe about Him, our Father is who He is. He longs for you to realize His true character and experience His love.

Further reading: Romans 3:23, Romans 6:23, Ephesians 2:8-9, 2 Corinthians 5:21

Your Father yearns for you to be His child.

Read: John 1:10-13

Turn back a few pages to the bold words in the introduction. This is the simplicity of the gospel. It's foundational for getting to know the Father because He doesn't force us to be adopted by Him. Rather, it is a conscious choice we have to make. Now, don't get me wrong. The Father has done everything in His power to make it possible for us to be His, but we have to take the final step. We have to believe Him and receive Him.

Did you know that your Father wanted to adopt you before you were even born? The entire Bible points to His plan to rescue us from sin and adopt us into His family. When a child is adopted, he or she bears the name of the adoptive family. Your Father claims you! He calls you His own! If you've agreed to the adoption, you belong to Him, and He belongs to you. Nothing in the world excites your Father more than hearing you call Him by name.

Further Reading: Romans 8:15, Galatians 4:4-6, Ephesians 1:5

Your Father is full of grace and truth. He has no room for evil!

Read: John 1:14-18

Have you ever known someone for a long time, admired them, and put them on a pedestal? Then eventually, as all people do, they disappointed you? There is not a single human on earth who has not sinned, and sin always disappoints someone. John wants us to know right off the bat that Jesus is completely full of grace and truth (verse 14) even though no other person ever has been.

The Greek word John used for "full" means perfect, lacking nothing, and every surface covered. Here is the fact: Jesus has no room in Him for evil! That means your Father will never do you wrong. Do you struggle to believe this? I did for a long time, but the more I've gotten to know Him, the more I trust that He is ALWAYS acting out of love for His children. To know Him is to trust Him!

Further reading: James 1:13, Mark 10:18

Your Father has been pursuing you for a long time to make you His child.

Read: John 1:19-28

Long before Jesus was born into this world, God sent a prophet named Isaiah to His people to encourage them. God had promised to send a Messiah to save them, and He even inspired Isaiah to point out the plan for someone to "make straight the way for the Lord" (Isaiah 40:3). When John the Baptist arrived on the scene, he was the fulfillment of that prophecy. He told the people God had made good on His promise to send someone to make the people ready to receive the Messiah, and the Messiah was soon to come.

It is no accident you are reading this book right now. Maybe you received it as a gift. Maybe you sought out a resource to help you grow closer to your Father. He intentionally sent this book your way because He desperately desires for you to enjoy being His child. He longs for you to know Him and trust Him. He went so far as to send the prophets of old, to send Jesus as Messiah for YOU, and then to inspire the writing of His Word in the Bible. He has taken every step toward you except the very last one. Step toward Him today. Make a commitment to finish what you have started to know your Father deeply and experience His love and longing for you.

Further Reading: Lamentations 3:22, 1 John 4:19

Your Father has a plan.

Read: John 1:29-34

God never intended to leave people guessing. He made sure it was clear that Jesus was the long awaited Messiah. The first of many signs came when John "saw the Spirit come down from heaven as a dove and remain on Him" (John 1:32). Remember, Jesus came to shed light on God's plan, not to confuse or frustrate us. God the Father wants us to understand who He is, why He sent Jesus, and how much He loves us.

In a similar way, the details of your life have not been accidental. Your parents may not have planned to have a child, but your Father made you on purpose. He's had His hand on you from conception. There has never been a season in your life when He was not involved. Hear me clearly. Your Father has doesn't make mistakes. He's never been surprised or caught off guard. He knows the best way to draw you to Himself. He has been lavishing His great love on you all along. Dear One, no matter how much we do not understand, His plans are trustworthy. Your Father is for you.

Further Reading: Jeremiah 29:11-13, Romans 1:2-4

Your Father gives you a name that provides life and meaning.

Read John 1:35-42

All of us take on an identity early in life based on the messages we receive from those around us. Maybe you wouldn't sign your journal with a name like *Forgotten* or *Worthless* or *Failure*, but many of us live out of such a name. Here's some good news for all of us. When Jesus called Simon to follow Him, He gave him a new name – Peter, which means Rock. Maybe Peter felt weak or unstable. We don't know, but Jesus called out the strength and immovability He knew was in Peter.

Your Father calls you by a name no one else may have ever called you. He tenderly calls His children *Beloved*, *Chosen*, *Forgiven*, *Holy*, *Beautiful*, and *Worthy*. Ask your Father to show you the name He would choose to call you – a name that will bring healing and hope and purpose to your life. The name He calls you matters more than any other. And who better to name you than the One who formed you in your mother's womb? He knows parts of your heart even you do not know. He calls out treasures you don't even know are there. And He can make your new name a reality. Why? Because He is your true Father.

Further Reading: Genesis 17:5, 15, Genesis 32:28, Judges 6:11-12, Isaiah 62:2, Revelation 2:17

Your Father sees you and knows you.

Read: John 1:43-51

When Jesus called Philip to follow Him, the first thing he did was go find his friend, Nathaniel. He couldn't NOT share Jesus with his pal! Nathaniel thought Jesus was from the wrong side of the tracks. He couldn't imagine anything good coming out of Jesus' hometown. When he met Jesus, he wasn't chided for being judgmental or not allowed to follow because he doubted. Jesus commented on Nathaniel's character to show how well He knew him, and then told him He saw him under the fig tree. I wonder what Nathaniel was doing under a fig tree. Was he praying? Was he having a conversation with someone else? Maybe he was thinking he could be invisible and no one would miss him? We don't know what Nathaniel was thinking or saying under the fig tree, but we do know that when he found out he was seen and cared about by Jesus, it made all the difference for him.

Do you ever feel unnoticed? Unnecessary even? Your Father sees everything in your life. He knows your heart, and He cares how you feel. You matter to Him more than you can even imagine. The conversation you have with yourself in your head…He hears. That voice that whispers to you when you lay in bed at night? He knows. All the work you do and the concerns you have? He sees. Take it all to Him so He can speak life into those places. You are important enough for Him to see and know.

Further Reading: Psalm 139:1-4, Hebrews 2:6

21

Your Father's timing can always be trusted.

Read: John 2:1-12

Jesus was thirty years old when He started His ministry of travelling, teaching, and healing. His timing was not arbitrary, nor was it accidental. The Father knows all things, and He knew the best time for Jesus to begin His ministry, how long it should last, and when He should reveal Himself as the Messiah. The Father has His hand in all the details of life. Nothing at all happens without His consent. He is seldom early, but never late.

Have you ever questioned God's timing only to realize later He had good reason? My husband and I are foster parents, and our licensing process took an unusually long time. We were frustrated with the wait, and then reminded that timing in foster care often determines the children we will receive into our home. If we were licensed earlier, we may have taken others and not been called for the ones who are now our own. If the process had taken longer, our little ones would have been placed elsewhere. In retrospect, we can see the Father's timing was perfect.

Are you in a season of waiting? You can trust your Father's timing. He is orchestrating the details of your life to accomplish His good will in you and through you. Surrender your wait to Him, and ask Him what He wants to show you in it. He can be trusted!

Further Reading: Psalm 25:3, Isaiah 40:31, John 11:5-6

Your Father's anger is always righteous.

Read: John 2:13-18

When Jesus arrived in Jerusalem to celebrate the Passover, He went to the Temple and found people making money by selling animals for the Passover sacrifice. He was angry because people had turned the Temple into a place for making a profit rather than a place to meet with God and worship Him. Wasn't Jesus right to be angry at the self-serving motives of those using the Temple courts? That was a sacred place, and one that held a special significance to Jesus.

I grew up thinking anger was a bad emotion, one I should never have. I thought anger was just a precursor to violence. Maybe you did, too. Yet Jesus' anger about merchants in the Temple was righteous. Your Father is certainly angry about injustice in this world. He hates when His children mistreat and hurt one another. Your Father is protective of you and always ready to defend you. He loves you so much that He doesn't miss a single moment of your life. He cares so deeply for you, Child. Rest under His watch today.

Further Reading: Psalm 7:6, Psalm 30:5, Psalm 36:6

Your Father is never surprised or shocked.

Read John 2:18-25

Jesus knew what was going to be done to Him before it ever happened. He knew His mission was to save mankind from eternal separation from the Father by sacrificing His life. He knew how His friends would treat Him: Peter would deny Him, Judas would betray Him, and Thomas would doubt Him. Yet He loved them and served them for three years, and then He laid down His very life for them.

In the same way, Your Father knew every mistake you would make before any of them happened. He knew every action even before you were born – the good, the bad, the ugly. Still, He delighted in making you. He delights in loving you and taking care of you. You don't ever have to worry that He will be shocked by your thoughts or what you do. You don't have to be concerned that His plans can't possibly move forward because of a roadblock. He saw it coming, and He devised His reaction before you even knew there was a problem. He will never be blindsided by circumstances or overwhelmed by the world. Stick with your Father, and you will never be lost. He's got this!

Further Reading: Genesis 6:12-14, Psalm 139:4, Matthew 26:75

Your Father is patient with you when you are confused.

Read: John 3:1-9

Nicodemus was a man with lots of questions, but he didn't want to be seen with Jesus. When he came to Jesus under the cover of night, Jesus was so patient with him. He listened and took time to explain and encourage. And just so you know, Nicodemus believed! He fell in love with Jesus and served Him (see John 19:39).

The Father can handle your questions. He *wants* you to bring your doubts to Him! Trust me, He can handle them. Do you have questions for your Father? Come to Him with each one. Then read His Word to search for answers. Surround yourself with His truth in Christian media and music, and godly relationships. Listen for the Holy Spirit to speak to your heart in His still, small voice. Your Father longs to have conversation with you. He will speak words of life to you.

Further Reading: Luke 1:34-35, Matthew 24:3

Your Father has used all of history to point you to Himself.

Read: John 3:9-15

Jews expected their savior would come as a military hero and save them from their enemies, but force and violence were never part of God's rescue plan. Jesus told Nicodemus that when Moses lifted up the snake in the wilderness (see Numbers 21:8-9), it was foreshadowing the way He would save His people. Before Moses and the Israelites ever needed the snake in the wilderness, God showed them how their lives could be saved by the blood of a perfect lamb (see Exodus 12:22-23). Even earlier in history, God had provided a lamb for Abraham to sacrifice in place of his son (see Genesis 22:7-14). He demonstrated for centuries that the blood of a "lamb" would save His people. That lamb would eventually be Jesus.

Think back on your own life. Are there events that point you to your Father? Do you see His hand of protection and the ways He has provided for you? How has He used your pain to draw you to Himself? How has He used nature to display His intimate involvement in your life? He had plans to save you even before He created the world. Believe it or not, your Father has been pursuing you all along. He has been using all of history to point you to Himself. He longs for you, Dear One. Reach out to Him today.

Further Reading: Psalm 19:1, Romans 8:28, Ephesians 3:9-11

Your Father desires to save, not condemn.

Read: John 3:16-21

I'm so glad John recorded Nicodemus' conversation with Jesus because his questions have been my questions as well. Growing up, I thought the Father was harsh and judgmental, and that I could never live up to His expectations. One of the most comforting verses in all of scripture is John 3:17, in which Jesus reminds us He did not come into the world to judge the world, but that we might be saved through Him. His desire for us is salvation!

Maybe you feel overwhelmed by your sin. Maybe you feel like the most awful person alive, and you want to hide your thoughts and actions from the rest of the world. I assure you, your Father is not ashamed to call you His own. His plan for you all along has been salvation. Before you were conceived, He knew you would need saving, and He made a way for that to happen. He loves you so much that He made a way to save you from the consequences of your sin so you can live in His presence both here on earth and for eternity. Oh, how your Father loves you!

Further Reading: John 8:10-11, Romans 8:33-34

Your Father wants you to know Him.

Read: John 3:22-34

Jesus didn't just appear on the scene with no introduction. Our Father didn't want anyone to miss the Messiah, so He sent John the Baptist ahead of Jesus to prepare the way. Even after Jesus arrived and John testified that He was the Messiah they had all been waiting for, John continued preaching as Jesus began His own ministry. Lots of people had questions about this Jesus, and the Father was wise enough to prepare John in advance to answer them.

John's message wasn't the only way your Father made His identity known. First, He sent the prophets of the Old Testament, then the disciples of the New Testament. He prompted forty authors on three continents over about 1500 years to write His words in the Bible so you and I could read them today. And He gave us the Holy Spirit to teach us and remind us who He is. Your Father has gone to such great lengths to show Himself to you and prove that He can be trusted. Thank Him today for bringing you to this journey of getting to know Him.

Further Reading: Psalm 119:27-28, Psalm 119:55, John 14:26

Your Father is angry about the pain and destruction that result from disobedience.

Read: John 3:34-36

I don't like to think of my Father as angry. In my mind, anger leads to violence, and I want Him to be jolly and happy and fun-loving all the time. However, when I come to Him with the pain that someone else has caused me, when I come to Him with injustice that disturbs me, I want Him to be an angry papa bear, defensive and protective of His own. I'm glad to know our Father doesn't pass off sin as no big deal. He is a good judge. I know my sin has hurt others, and their sin has hurt me, and our Father can't stand the pain and destruction it has caused.

Your Father isn't angry with you. Dear One, you may need to read that one more time. Your Father is NOT angry with you. He loves you so much that He is brokenhearted by the devastation that comes with disobeying Him. He longs for so many good things for you. Your Father knows that obeying Him leads to peace and joy for you and others around you. Moreover, He will make right everything that has been done to you. He is defensive for His own, and He is for you.

Further Reading: Psalm 32:1, Psalm 99:8, Romans 8:32

Your Father initiates relationship.

Read: John 4:1-9

Jesus sat by a well in Samaria in the afternoon sun when a Samaritan woman came to draw water. She was known around town as a sinner. She came alone to draw water instead of coming with the rest of the women early in the morning. She was not the fine, upstanding citizen everyone wanted around. But none of that mattered to Jesus. The woman was shocked when He asked her for a drink. She knew Jews hated Samaritans. She knew it was not socially appropriate for a man to speak to a woman in public who was not his wife. She also knew she had not lived the kind of life worthy of this man's respect.

It does not matter what your life has looked like thus far. It doesn't even matter if your life is a mess today. Your Father has been pursuing you when you didn't know it and when you didn't deserve it. He loves you that much. He initiated your relationship with Him. You are not reading this book by accident. He is drawing you to Himself, revealing Himself purposely to you, so He can enjoy being your Father as much as you can enjoy being His child. You are worth His pursuit!

Further Reading: Romans 5:8, 1 John 4:19

Your Father brings up the past to heal, not to condemn.

Read: John 4:10-18

When Jesus met the woman at the well, He saw great need. He knew her history and her regrets and her pain. He knew she needed great healing. Yet to begin that healing process, Jesus brought up her history. Why? Was He being unkind? Judgmental? No. Sometimes we have to look at our past in the face to receive healing. Jesus brought the woman's past into the conversation because He wanted to heal her (see her happy, relieved, excited reaction in John 4:28-29). Jesus spoke the hard truth, but He didn't shame her for it or lecture her about it.

Your Father doesn't want to shame you or lecture you, either. He desires to face your past with you, show you where He was working in the middle of it, and heal you from its devastating consequences. Your Father is the safest person with whom you can talk about the deepest, darkest secrets of your heart. Remember, you cannot shock Him. You never have to be embarrassed with Him. Only He can bring you the healing you are longing for. Trust Him with your past. He can handle it.

Further Reading: Isaiah 61:1-4, Luke 4:16-21

Your Father doesn't seek worship; He seeks worshippers.

Read: John 4:19-26

The woman at the well changed the subject quickly when Jesus brought up her past. Jesus was so gentle, He followed her lead and answered her questions, but His answers continually directed her to the truth that worship dictates everything in our lives. Our race and religion and social status don't change that. We were made to worship, and we all worship something all the time. Some of us worship ourselves, seeking pleasure above all else. Some of us worship our identity in a career or financial standing. Some of us even worship control, trying desperately to have our hands in every detail in every situation. (I'm especially guilty of that one.)

Your Father knows that worshipping Him changes everything. He doesn't need our worship. He isn't any less God if we don't worship Him, but we lose out on an abundance of blessings if we make something or someone else the object of our devotion. Your Father wants good things for you. He wants the fruit of His Spirit to characterize your life as you love Him above all other things. How can you worship Him with your life today?

Further Reading: Exodus 34:14, 1 Samuel 15:22, Psalm 95:6

Your Father chooses the most unlikely people.

Read John 4:27-38

Jesus could not possibly speak to every person when He walked this earth because, in His human body, He was bound by time and space. His strategy was to pour into people who would then pour into others. I love that He didn't just choose wealthy, religious, educated people to share His message. He chose a Samaritan woman, full of the stains of sin and regret, to tell her people about Him. Jesus chose a band of misfit disciples who were mostly uneducated, smelly fisherman. One was a despised tax collector. He even chose a man he knew would eventually betray Him to His death.

The Father chooses to use ordinary people like you and me to accomplish His mission. As His children, He doesn't want us deciding we can do many things *for* Him. He wants us to listen and just do the things He tells us. That takes so much pressure off of those of us who want to try to save the whole world! We can rest in the fact that our Father is God, and we are not. He knows what each person on earth needs, and He can handle the details of meeting those needs through anyone He chooses. Your life has incredible significance. Rejoice today in the fact that your Father has chosen you to be part of His mission.

Further Reading: 2 Samuel 7:18-22, 1 Chronicles 29:14, Acts 4:13

Your Father has a heart for those who are despised.

Read: John 4:39-43

Jesus was a cultural and religious Jew. The rest of the Jews in His day despised the Samaritans. They were considered "half-breeds", the result of Jewish people intermarrying with pagans. In fact, when Jews travelled, they would intentionally take the long way around a Samaritan city just so they could avoid them. But not Jesus. He took His disciples to a place other Jews would not go. He spoke kindly with a Samaritan woman. He respected her people, and the people responded by asking Him to stay with them — which He did for two more days.

Have you been rejected? Maybe you feel like it was your fault. Maybe you don't. Regardless, your Father has a heart for those who are despised by others. Maybe your spouse constantly criticizes you. Not your Father. Maybe the church has ostracized you because of your past. Not your Father. Maybe people look down on you because of your race, family, status, or social standing. Not your Father. He accepts you as you are. You don't have to change a thing to come to Him. He is crazy about you! When you receive the acceptance He offers, you will ask Him to stay.

Further Reading: Mark 2:14-17, Mark 14:3-9

Your Father has compassion on those who are hurting or fearful.

Read John 4:43-54

There is nothing that makes a person hurt more or worry more than a deathly sick child. There was a royal official in Cana who had this predicament. It's interesting to note that this man probably didn't know much about Jesus except that He was a miracle-worker. People sometimes came to Jesus for purely selfish reasons, and Jesus still had such compassion on them. The official begged Jesus to save the life of his son, and Jesus was happy to oblige.

Are you hurting or fearful? Your Father not only understands, He also has compassion on you. He desires to heal your pain. Believe Him that He can, and you will be amazed at how much He changes things. Sometimes He changes *you* more than He changes circumstances, but either way will be healing for your soul. You can trust His sweet compassion.

Further Reading: 2 Chronicles 30:9, Nehemiah 9:19, Psalm 103:8

Your Father will meet you wherever you are.

Read: John 5:1-4

At first glance, it doesn't seem so odd that Jesus would go to the pool at Bethesda. However, that particular pool was a pagan sanitarium dedicated to Asclepius, the Greek god of medicine. It was a pool with five porticoes and about 16 million gallons of water. Thanks to a marginal note added by a scribe writing down the gospel of John, we know the superstition surrounding the pool. Apparently, some people believed an angel would periodically come down and stir the water, and the first person to win the race into the pool would be healed. This pool was a tragic symbol of false hope for many with infirmities, not a place where any "good" Jew would have gone.

Your Father is willing to pursue you anywhere, be it your family's house, a church house, a crack house, or a whore house. He loves you right where you are and is relentless in His pursuit of you. Maybe you think you are in a place where He would never go. You're mistaken. He is right there with you, drawing you to Himself. Just listen for His call.

Further Reading: Psalm 139:7-12, Jeremiah 23:23-24

Your Father is a Healer.

Read John 5:5-9

Imagine a man, thirty-eight years lame, who had lost all hope of ever walking. When Jesus shows up on the scene, the man doesn't even ask for healing. He has given up. He didn't know Jesus had been healing in ways no one else ever had before. Jesus healed the man even though he didn't ask. Even though he didn't believe. Jesus had compassion on him and healed him.

Your Father is a Healer. It's what He does. It's who He is. There is never a moment when healing is not in His plan. We may not see physical healing this side of Heaven as the man at the pool did, but that doesn't change the fact that your Father is *always* healing. His healing is so thorough that He changes physical, emotional, and spiritual circumstances. He is wise in His choices with regards to healing. He knows what you need most. He can be trusted to heal you perfectly.

Further Reading: Malachi 4:2, Matthew 9:35, Luke 6:19, Acts 10:38

Your Father is concerned for your wellbeing.

Read: John 5:9-14

After Jesus healed the man at the pool at Bethesda, He found him later at the Temple. Jesus knew the man needed something more important than the healing that made him able to walk. Jesus said to him, "Behold, you have become well; do not sin anymore so that nothing worse happens to you." Sin wreaks havoc in our lives more than any physical ailment ever could. Jesus is concerned for us to be righteous because He knows the devastating effects of sin, and He does not want that for us.

Your Father wants you to spend eternity with Him. He knows, deep down, that's what your soul longs for most of all, too. However, He also desires intimacy with you here on earth, and He knows that sin eventually brings nothing but loneliness and misery. He wants you to have no place for ongoing sin in your life because He wants good things for you! Your Father's heart is concerned for you, His precious child. Trust Him because He knows what is best for you. I promise.

Further Reading: Psalm 107:10-16, Psalm 119:71-72

Your Father never stops working to give you life.

Read: John 5:15-24

The religious leaders of Jesus' day had some strange ideas about what was considered "work." They took God's rule – to keep the Sabbath Day holy – and made it into many rules. They even considered Jesus healing a man to be work! When they confronted Jesus about healing on the Sabbath, He informed them that as God's Son, He would continue working as long as the Father was working.

Your Father is continually laboring on your behalf because He wants you to have abundant life. Others may label you as needy or difficult, but you're never an inconvenience to your Father. He never needs a break from you, so He's happy to help you and spend time with you – even on weekends and holidays when everyone else wants the day off. Ask Him what His abundant life looks like for you today.

Further Reading: John 10:10, Psalm 36:7-9, Psalm 121:3-4

Your Father's will is best.

Read: John 5:25-30

Many times I've questioned the Father's will in my life. I have often been unhappy with my own set of circumstances. I've confused His will with people's free choice. It can be a very difficult concept, but here are two things I've learned. First, if Jesus agreed that the Father's plan was best and submitted to Him, then I can trust Him enough to do the same. There were plenty of instances in Jesus' life when He could have said, "Father, is this really the plan?" He even agonized over that question in the Garden of Gethsemene (Matthew 26:39), but never once did He refuse to obey. Jesus followed the Father fully because He trusted Him fully.

The second truth I've learned about the Father's will is that it always begins right where you are. His will for you doesn't begin when you turn forty or when you get your act together or when you get married. His will for you starts when and where you are right now. We know for sure He wants to be your Father, and He longs for you to relate to Him as His child. That is where His will for you starts...right now.

Further Reading: Mark 14:36, Romans 12:2, 1 Peter 2:15, 2 Peter 3:9

Your Father's actions prove who He is.

Read: John 5:31-40

Have you ever known someone who put their best foot forward when you met, only to find out later they weren't who you thought they were? I have. Sometimes we fail to trust our Father because the people in our own lives have been untrustworthy, but we don't have to have *blind* faith in Jesus. John the Baptist testified to His identity. Jesus' miracles and teaching confirm for us that He was God in the flesh. God the Father even spoke audibly on at least three occasions to confirm that Jesus was who He said He was. Furthermore, the prophecies of the Old Testament that were fulfilled in Jesus give us overwhelming evidence that God our Father came to earth in the person of Jesus to save us from our sins.

The final proof of the Father's love for you is the fact that He willingly died to pay the penalty for your sins! How many people do you know who would die for you? Your Father loves you so much He would rather die than live without you. Stop and read that again. Your Father loves you so much He would rather die than live without you. You are totally worth it to Him. All the blood, sweat, and tears He has cried on your behalf – they are all worth it. He wouldn't give up on you for the whole world. Rest today in knowing that you are worth it to your Father – whatever it takes.

Further Reading: John 10:17-18, Romans 5:6-8

Your Father wants you to care about His opinion above all others.

Read: John 5:41-47

Jesus' main complaint against the Jewish religious leaders was their pious way of showing off their religiosity for the world to see. Their own pride blinded them to the truth. It was more important to them to look good for everyone around them than for God to be pleased with their heart. Think about your own life. Are you living to impress someone? Is your highest goal to produce well-behaved children, smart students in your classroom, or the best team at work because they are all a reflection of you?

Your Father is drawn to humility and honesty. He honors the person who is vulnerable and asks for help. He doesn't want you pretending like you have it all together. He holds in high esteem His child who admits to being broken and flawed and desires His intervention. Our culture does not value weakness and vulnerability, but your Father does. If He is prompting you to be vulnerable and expose your secrets to a trusted friend or mentor, I would encourage you not to wait. Your Father is honored by your real, genuine transparency. And He is proud to call you His own!

Further Reading: Psalm 51:16-17, James 4:6

Your Father is not deterred by few resources.

Read: John 6:1-10

As Jesus healed many people of physical, emotional, and spiritual maladies, huge crowds began to follow Him. One day, they were all out on the hillside with nothing to eat. Jesus asked His disciples, "Well, boys, what do you think we should do?" He already knew the plan, but He wanted to see what they would come up with. I can just see Him grinning ear to ear as they stumbled over their words trying to make sense of the question. Andrew brought to Jesus the only resources available – a meager two fish and five small pieces of bread. That would have discouraged me, but Jesus didn't change His plans because they had no means to pull it off. He just used what they had.

Your Father is not concerned by your lack of finances or self-control or life experience. He's an expert at working miracles with what little you have. That's why He gave us the Holy Spirit – to make up for our deficiencies. Take to your Father all you have – a broken heart, a dead-end job, ruined relationships, or fragments of a shattered life. I know from experience He makes the most beautiful stained glass out of the most broken pieces.

Further Reading: Psalm 50:10-12, Genesis 1:2-3

Your Father loves to go beyond just meeting a need.

Read: John 6:9-13

After Jesus multiplied the two fish and five pieces of bread to feed five thousand men (plus women and children), there were twelve baskets full of the leftovers. He didn't feed everyone just enough to get by. He made enough food to fill them all to the brim, and then made sure there were leftovers. Jesus loved the crowds lavishly, providing abundantly more than they needed.

Your Father also loves to go beyond just meeting your needs. It puts a smile on His face to see His child enjoying a good gift from Him. Maybe you don't ask your Father to meet your needs because you don't think you deserve it. Your worthiness really doesn't matter to your Father. His grace is based on His character, not yours. He is a good Father who loves to give good gifts. Enjoy His good gifts today.

Further Reading: James 1:17, Romans 6:23

Your Father is perceptive, not easily distracted or oblivious.

Read: John 6:14-15

Jesus remained focused on the mission. He knew the people wanted to take Him by force to make Him king, but that wasn't the plan, so He stole away by Himself. Jesus perceived in the hearts of the people even what they did not express out loud. This sensitivity is comforting for anyone who feels forgotten or overlooked by the world.

Even if you seem invisible to everyone else, you are not invisible to your Father. Not only does He see your physical person, He sees your heart. Even if there are a thousand distractions around you, and a million other people who need His help, He still pays attention to you. He notices where you are and what you are doing. He is not oblivious to your emotions or your desires. He always has time for you. Enjoy a little extra time alone with your Father today. He will enjoy it too.

Further Reading: Psalm 94:7-9, Luke 8:46-47

Your Father never sets out to frighten His children. He wants you to feel safe with Him.

Read: John 6:16-21

When evening came, Jesus had not come down from the mountain to which He had escaped the people who wanted to force Him to be king. So the disciples got into a boat to go to the other side of the sea. During their journey, a storm came up, and Jesus came to them walking on the water. However, He wasn't like a bullying big brother who enjoys scaring his sisters at night. On the contrary, even before He arrived at the boat, He called out to let them know it was Him.

Have you lived your life afraid of the wrath or condescension of your Father? Have you been afraid He would bully and abuse you or humiliate you? These fears indicate a lack of understanding of just who your Father really is. To know Him is to trust Him! I'll say that one more time. To know Him is to trust Him! I promise He is not like any earthly father, even the best of them. He is in a league all His own, characterized by lavish love and amazing grace. Tell your Father what scares you about Him. I did. He can handle our doubts and fears, and even use them to draw us closer to Himself.

Further Reading: Deuteronomy 7:9, Psalm 103:6-13

Your Father has an eternal perspective.

Read: John 6:22-27

Jesus knew the hearts of the people who followed Him across the sea. He knew they wanted another free meal, so He reminded them that food is not the most important thing in this life. He wanted them to focus on working for what would last. So then, what is this "food that remains to eternal life – the food which the Son of Man will give to you (verse 27)?" The answer is relationship. That's what changes eternity. Relationship with Jesus and relationship with people.

Your Father wants to help you focus on what will last. He wants you working toward leaving a legacy that points people to Him. What are you pouring your time and energy into right now? Does it connect you more to your Father or people around you? People are what matter most to your Father. You don't have to impress Him with a beautiful house or fancy car. You don't have to produce anything on earth that the world says you should. Focus your time and attention on your Father, and He will emphasize what is most important for you.

Further Reading: Ecclesiastes 3:11, Ephesians 5:15-16

Your Father invites you to join Him in His work by believing.

Read: John 6:27-29

Have you ever wanted to change the world but don't have a clue where to start? Jesus gave us an interesting answer to that predicament. He said, "This is the work of God, that you believe in Him whom He has sent." That word *believe* is one of my favorites in all of scripture. It comes from the original Greek word, *pisteuo*, which means "to have faith in a person or entrust one's self to a person." This, Jesus said, is how we join the Father in His work and change the world.

How do you entrust yourself to the Father? *Pisteuo* gives me the mental picture of a walker. An elderly or disabled person puts all her weight on this device (trusts it to hold her up) so she can move forward. That's what it means to entrust yourself to your Father. Put all your weight on Him, lean on Him with all you've got, and continue moving forward. Your Father can be trusted. He won't let you fall.

Further Reading: Acts 16:31, 1 Peter 2:23

Your Father meets needs you don't even know you have.

Read: John 6:29-36

When the crowd asked Jesus for a meal, He told them they were being short-sighted. When they asked Him how to join the Father in His work, He told them they needed to entrust themselves to Him. When they asked Jesus for a sign that they should listen to Him and believe, He told them the Father provided Himself as the Bread of Life. The people didn't even know they needed the Bread of Life! They just knew they could use a little bread to fill their bellies.

Your Father knows you have needs that you don't even know about. In fact, as is characteristic of children, we often ask for something our Father knows would be detrimental to us. (Have your kids ever asked you to feed them candy for breakfast, lunch, and dinner?) Even if He has to say no, Your Father is pleased by the fact you have faith enough to ask Him. He can be trusted to meet your needs, even if you don't know what that looks like. Take all your needs to Him. He is there waiting for you.

Further Reading: Matthew 6:8, Luke 11:11-13

Your Father will never cast away the one who comes to Him.

Read: John 6:37

Jesus told the crowd in plain words a foundational truth that could change your life. He promised anyone who comes humbly to Him will not be cast away. He doesn't insist we clean up our act or figure out the Bible first. He doesn't give us a to-do-list before we can come to Him. He simply says, "Come."

Do you ever cover your face when you are ashamed? Do you avoid people who you think have it all together? Do you hide from situations that remind you of your regrets? You don't have to do any of this with your Father. He already knows everything you have done and everything you will do. He is proud to call you His child, and He wants you to come to Him confidently. His love is enough to cover all sin. His grace is enough to redeem any situation. He will never, ever, ever cast you away when you come to Him. He loves you more than you can imagine!

Further Reading: Luke 15:11-24, Hebrews 4:15-16

Your Father's goal is always restoration, life, and relationship with His children.

Read: John 6:38-47

The religious leaders were grumbling about Jesus calling Himself the One who came down out of heaven. Jesus answered them (even though they didn't ask Him anything) because He knew what they were thinking. He explained that the Father desires for His children to be raised up to live with Him forever. They didn't understand, so He told them again that "he who believes has eternal life." I wonder if Nicodemus was in that group of religious leaders and thought back to the conversation he had with Jesus that night when Jesus told him, "God did not send the Son into the world to judge the world, but that the world might be saved through Him."

This always has been and always will be the goal of your Father. He has desired to restore His relationship with His children since they left the Garden of Eden. The entire Old Testament points to the Father's plan to rescue His children by sending Jesus to pay the penalty for their sin. Those of us on this side of the cross can enjoy unbroken fellowship with the Father because of Jesus' sacrifice. Thank Him today for restoring you in relationship with Him and giving you life again.

Further Reading: John 3:17, Matthew 18:12-14

Your Father is willing to talk about tough stuff.

Read: John 6:48-65

This is, for many people, a very uncomfortable passage of scripture. Jesus isn't condoning cannibalism. Rather, He's making a reference to the sacrifice He would become to pay for the sins of the world. When the Israelites were enslaved in Egypt and God sent ten plagues, He told them to kill and eat a Passover lamb so the Angel of Death would "pass over" their homes and spare them (Exodus 12:8). So eating the flesh of the Passover lamb literally saved them. Jesus came to be our Passover lamb (John 1:29).

Jesus didn't give this explanation to the religious leaders, knowing that the Holy Spirit would connect the dots after His resurrection. He simply spoke truth. The Father is always willing to speak hard truth, even if we don't get it right away. He understands all things, so He's willing to talk about the tough stuff that feels too awkward to bring up. He doesn't shy away from uncomfortable conversations. Bring Him all your questions and doubts, all your worries and fears, all your past and present struggles. No subject is off limits for Him.

Further Reading: Psalm 139, Isaiah 40:28

Your Father has what you need.

Read: John 6:66-69

After Jesus had a difficult conversation with the religious leaders about eating His flesh and drinking His blood, "many of His disciples withdrew and were not walking with Him anymore" (vs. 66). When Jesus asked if any of the Twelve wanted to leave as well, Peter told Him there was no one to whom they could turn. No one else could offer what He did. This is a true statement in every area of life.

Your Father is the answer for your relationship issues, your addiction, your fear, your illness. Yes, He uses the wisdom He has given to doctors and therapists, but we must acknowledge our help comes from Him. Go to Him first when you are struggling. Go to Him first when you want to celebrate good things! Go to Him first when you are confused or bored or frustrated or depressed. He will give you guidance to know where to go from there. Just go to Him first, because no one but your Father has what you need the most.

Further Reading: Psalm 54:4, Psalm 121:1-2

Your Father is in control, even when bad things happen.

Read: John 6:70-71

Why do bad things happen to good people? This is an age old question that theologians have wrestled with for centuries. Jesus pointed out to His twelve disciples that He knowingly chose one of them who would betray Him to His death. Why would Jesus do that? The answer is in the gospel. Jesus knew what must happen in order for you and me to be saved. No one took His life from Him; He willingly laid it down for us. He never lost control of the situation for one moment.

Have you ever thought God couldn't be all-loving and all-powerful at the same time because of the circumstances in your life? I know I have. Here is a truth that changes everything: Your Father will never allow something to happen that He can't use for the good of His children. He promised. He has never broken a promise. He is never the author of sin or suffering, but if He allows tragedy and hardship in your life, you can rest assured He will use it for good. He is always acting out of love. Ask Him to give you His perspective on bad things. Then enjoy the peace that comes from knowing your Father is always in control.

Further Reading: Genesis 50:20, Psalm 46:10, Matthew 26:50-54, Romans 8:28

Your Father's presence will expose and discourage evil.

Read: John 7:1-9

Jesus said, "[The world] hates Me because I testify of it, that its deeds are evil." I feel like evil is on the rise in our world. (That's probably because the media loves to report tragedy and negativity because it keeps people fearfully watching.) Some days, I feel overwhelmed by all the wickedness. I wonder what kind of evils my children will one day face. I worry that our faith won't be strong enough to withstand them, but then I remember we know how the story ends.

I know our Father wins the war. I am on the winning side. I want to be found with the One whose very presence exposes and discourages evil. That's the best place to be in a world like this. In a time when wickedness runs rampant, Your Father offers a place of safety and security. His perfection sheds light on anyone or anything that is not of Him, and He invites you into His very own presence where evil cannot remain. Let's look forward to the day when our tiny glimpses of that heavenly place here on earth will be eclipsed by an eternity where evil is no more.

Further Reading: Psalm 91:1-16

Your Father is the source of knowledge and wisdom.

Read: John 7:8-17

Jesus was wise to lay low at the Festival of Tabernacles. He hid Himself until halfway through the celebration because the religious leaders wanted to kill Him. Finally, Jesus went up to the temple to teach, and the Jews were amazed by His knowledge and wisdom, especially considering He had never been formally educated. The religious leaders were considered some of the most educated people in society, and even they were amazed by Jesus. There seemed to be nothing He didn't know something about. There was no question they could ask Him for which He didn't have a wise answer.

There are many tasks I do and relationships I have that make me wish I had formal training for them. Isn't it comforting to know that any wisdom we need, our Father has it? What decisions in your life require divine knowledge and wisdom today? Take them to your Father. He has given you the Holy Spirit to teach you all you need to know.

Further Reading: Proverbs 9:10, John 14:26, James 1:5-6

Your Father does not judge by appearances.

Read: John 7:18-24

Jesus wasn't so interested in behavior. He was interested in the heart. He called out the religious leaders who were inconsistent in their argument about not working on the Sabbath. They made exceptions for themselves, but not for anyone else. Jesus saw their hearts, which were legalistic and far from the Father. The religious leaders were all about appearances, making sure everyone else looked bad enough to make them look good.

Your Father does not judge you by how "put together" your life looks. (I'm so grateful!) He does not care if your house looks "right" and your clothes fit "right" and your kids act "right". Your Father cares about what is in your heart. He desires your willingness to obey, and your humility that allows you to ask for forgiveness when you have been wrong. He wants your honesty. He wants your heart. Ask Him to search your heart now and show you what He sees. Remember, He brings up issues to heal you, not condemn you. He is gentle and kind when you come humbly to Him. He is so safe.

Further Reading: Isaiah 29:13, Psalm 139:23-24

Your Father is sovereign, and nothing can happen which He does not allow.

Read: John 7:25-36

Jesus knew the religious leaders wanted to kill Him even though they denied it. He also knew the Father had a plan for when He was to lay down His life, and He knew it wasn't time yet. That's why He was able to speak publicly and be out and about. Jesus knew the Father was in control, even of the Jews who wanted to kill Him. He kept His eyes not on the cross to come, but on the victory.

In His sovereignty, your Father has given all people free will. However, He retains the power to intervene in any person and any situation. We may not understand why He allows some things and not others, but He can be trusted. He promised He will never allow anything that He can't use for your good and His glory (Romans 8:28). We will never know until we get to Heaven every situation in which He has protected us. If you struggle to trust Him because of what He has allowed to happen in your life, ask Him to show you where He was and what He was doing at that time. Ask Him humbly how He is accomplishing His promise to use the bad for good. The Holy Spirit can show you if you listen carefully to Him.

Further Reading: Genesis 50:20, Psalm 103:19

Your Father wants to quench every thirst.

Read: John 7:37-39

During the traditional Jewish Feast of Booths, there was a water-drawing ceremony each day for seven days, which reached a climax on the last day. This is probably what was happening when Jesus called out, "If anyone is thirsty, let him come to Me and drink." The people were crowded around, following the processional of the water being carried from the Pool of Siloam to the Temple. Along the way, they celebrated God's great provision. Unbeknownst to them, Jesus was the ultimate provision of God the Father for His children.

What do you thirst for? What is your deepest desire? Love? Significance? Healing? Peace? Your Father wants to quench every thirst you have. He alone can fulfill your deepest desires and your greatest longings. Go to Him with your thirst today, and let Him satisfy you in the depths of your soul.

Further Reading: Psalm 37:4, Romans 8:32, John 4:13-14

Your Father speaks in a different way than anyone else.

Read: John 7:40-53

There was a lot of division among the people – and even among the religious leaders – over Jesus. The prophets had said the Messiah would come from Bethlehem, but the people didn't realize that's where Jesus was born. However, they couldn't discount the fact that He was different than anyone else they had ever met. He spoke differently. He acted differently. No one could find fault with Him. Even non-religious people wanted to be around Him. People felt safe with Him and hung on His every word.

This is who your Father is. He is kind and gentle and safe. He has the kind of personality that draws people to Him. He has a smile and laugh that invites even children to chase Him. Your Father will never speak to you the way some people have spoken to you. His motive is always love. He gently pursues you, earning your trust every step of the way. Beloved, Keep looking to Him and getting to know Him because to know Him is to trust Him.

Further Reading: Matthew 7:28-29, Matthew 19:14

Your Father considers your relationship more important than sleep.

Read: John 7:53-8:1

After Jesus finished teaching in the temple, "everyone went to his home, but Jesus went to the Mount of Olives." That was one of His favorite places to meet with the Father. It was more important to Him to spend time communing with the Father than to find a place to sleep. He prioritized time with the Father every day over everything else. Even with all the important work He had to do and all the people who needed His touch, Jesus started and ended His days with the Father.

Do you feel like life is too busy to spend time with your Father? He doesn't feel like life is too busy to spend time with you. Have you ever realized how much He treasures your time together? He waits eagerly for you to spend time with Him. He enjoys your company! No one on earth will ever want to be with you more than your Father wants to be with you. Give Him some extra time today. Find a cozy spot to sit quietly and imagine Him sitting next to you with His arm around you. If you can't trust Him enough yet to have His arm around you, He would be content to sit with you and not touch you. Remember, He is gentle and kind and safe. He will give you all the time you need to learn to trust Him. He loves you!

Further Reading: Psalm 5:3, Mark 1:35

Your Father doesn't condemn. He desires to help you leave a life of sin.

Read: John 8:2-11

This story shows one of my very favorite pictures of the Father. An adulterous woman had been caught in the very act, and was no doubt half-dressed and humiliated in front of a crowd of people. When she was brought to Jesus, he didn't tower over her, or even stand face-to-face to stare at her. He stooped down in a non-threatening way and began writing in the dirt on the ground. When the religious leaders pressed Him for a verdict, He stood and called them out on their own sin. Then He bent down again, not even looking at the woman, who was so embarrassed she could not stand to be looked at. How kind Jesus was to her! After everyone else left and He was alone with the woman, only then did He stand and look her in the eye. He told her gently He did not condemn her. What a beautiful picture of grace! Then He encouraged her, after all He had done for her, to go and sin no more.

Your Father knows your embarrassment. He knows your pain. He is not threatening or domineering. He is not shaming you or blaming you. He loves you enough to tell you He does not condemn you. He wants to help you leave your life of sin because He knows how painful and shameful that life is. He gets down to your level and speaks tenderly to you as a Father to a young child. He is for you! Receive His gentle words of grace to you today.

Further Reading: Romans 2:4, Romans 8:1

Your Father speaks up for His children and claims them.

Read: John 8:12-18

The Father desires for our relationship with Him to look like the relationship He had with Jesus on earth (John 17:26). The Father claimed Jesus no matter what other people thought of Him. Jesus knew He was loved and accepted whether the crowds were cheering Him or trying to run Him out of town. He was secure in the Father's love, and He desires for us to be as well.

Maybe you've been rejected, ostracized from your family or your church. Your Father will never reject you. He speaks up for you and claims you. He's proud to be called your Father. He smiles when He hears you speak His name. He's elated to know He is earning your trust. Nothing in the world makes Him more proud than His precious children – and that includes you, Dear One.

Further Reading: Psalm 27:10, Isaiah 49:15-16

Your Father revealed Himself perfectly in Jesus.

Read: John 8:19

Dear Child, this is a good time to remind you that Jesus is the perfect picture of your Father with all His emotion, His mannerisms, and His contagious joy. Meditate on Jesus' kindness and gentleness, His tenderness and compassion, His wisdom, and His healing touch. Everything that has caused you to fall in love with Him shows you exactly what your Father is like. Oh, how He yearns for you to know Him and trust Him.

Take a few moments to think back over the last few weeks you've been reading this daily devotional. How has your view of your Father changed? Do you know Him better now? Can you trust Him more now than you did before? I pray that your trust will continue to grow as you linger in John's gospel, studying the life of Jesus. Thank Him today for giving you such a vivid picture of your Father.

Further Reading: Hebrews 1:3, John 10:30

Your Father warns you of what is to come so you may be saved.

Read: John 8:20-27

Some people think it's harsh to tell others they cannot be saved if they don't believe in Jesus. Some people think it's judgmental to warn others of the dangers of Hell. Jesus' motivation was never punitive or cruel. He always spoke and acted out of love. He plainly told the religious leaders He could save them if they believed Him, but they refused. He says the same to us as well. He doesn't call us terrible people or shame us for our sinfulness. He simply tells the truth. We are sinners in need of a Savior, and our Father provided that Savior for us.

If my little girl was running toward the street into the path of an on-coming car, it would not be loving or tolerant of me to keep my mouth shut. How much worse is eternal separation from the Father than physical death here on earth! Your Father has warned you of the dangers of sin and pride and self-sufficiency because He loves you. He has been willing to speak truth to you because He wants you saved, not just from Hell, but from the loneliness that results when we do not trust Him. Your Father is trustworthy, Dear One. He will do whatever it takes to reach you.

Further Reading: Joshua 1:7-8, Psalm 119:9-11, Psalm 119:105

Your Father doesn't leave His children alone…ever.

Read: John 8:28-30

Jesus knew bad things were going to happen to Him. He knew the people would call for Him to be crucified. He knew He would endure an incredible amount of pain, but He never doubted that the Father was with Him. Jesus knew the Father would never leave Him on His own. No matter what life looked like, and no matter how badly He was treated, He was confident in the Father's enduring presence and everlasting love.

I bet we have all wondered at one time or another, "God, where were You when…?" When life is hard and we are mistreated, the enemy loves to tell us our Father has left us and doesn't care anymore. That couldn't be further from the truth. Your Father will never leave you, no matter what. Think back on your life and look for His fingerprints in the most difficult seasons. Was there a godly friend there to encourage you? Did you hear a song on the radio that spoke truth to you? Was there safety in the midst of turmoil? Is it possible your Father protected you from something tragic you don't even know about? No matter what season of life you are thinking of right now, your Father was there, loving you all along.

Further Reading: Deuteronomy 31:8, Joshua 1:9, Hebrews 13:5-6

Your Father wants His children to be free.

Read John 8:31-36

Jesus told people they needed freedom when they didn't even understand they were enslaved. Freedom was His dream for those people – freedom from sin, from addiction, from people-pleasing, from legalism, from fear. What keeps you enslaved these days? What area of your life causes you to long for freedom?

I used to be a slave to fear and a victim mentality. I didn't even realize I was craving freedom until my Father showed me. He told me He wanted me to be free. Your Father desperately wants you to be free, too. That's why He tells you the truth. His truth is what sets you free. Your Father won't blackmail you or try to control you. He's not manipulative or coercive. He wants you to love Him of your own free will. He wants you to desire time with Him because you have experienced the depths of His love. What lies are you hearing today that threaten your liberty? Ask your Father to reveal His truth that will set you free.

Further Reading: Romans 8:1-4, 2 Corinthians 3:17, Galatians 5:13, 1 Peter 2:16

Your Father is speaking, even when you aren't listening.

Read: John 8:37-47

Jesus had been teaching the religious leaders and the crowds about who He was for weeks. Yet, their preconceived notions prevented them from understanding and receiving His truth. Jesus was not the Messiah they expected. Even though most people refused His message, He kept right on teaching and healing. He continued to reveal the Father, even when many refused to listen.

My own expectations of the Father prevented me from trusting Him enough to listen. Do you avoid your Father because of your fear? Even now, He is bringing you face to face with who He *really* is. What will you do with what He's saying to you? Will you listen and take Him at His word? Will you believe Him after all the ways He's proven Himself? Will you dare to draw near to Him? Talk to your Father about where your heart is right now. Tell Him how you're feeling and what you want to say to Him. He'll always listen to you. Then, take time to listen to Him, too. He is speaking.

Further Reading: Psalm 19:1-3, Matthew 6:26, John 5:25

Your Father does not answer violence with violence.

Read: John 8:47-59

Jesus continued debating with the Jews about His identity day after day. They understood He was claiming to be God Himself when He said, "Before Abraham was born, I AM" (see Exodus 3:14). For that reason, the Jews sought to stone Jesus to death. I can assure you that He hid Himself, not out of fear, but because He does not answer violence with violence. In fact, the Jewish people had hoped their Messiah would be a military man who would fight for them against the Romans. Yet Jesus was peaceable, gentle, and approachable.

Your Father is peaceable, gentle, and approachable. He is not easily angered, and He is not violent. You may have had experience with an earthly father who was irritable and violent. Your Father is not this way. Come in to His open arms today, and rest in His peaceful, gentle embrace.

Further Reading: Psalm 86:5, Psalm 86:15, Psalm 103:8

Your Father notices just one person.

Read: John 9:1

In this verse, Jesus has a lot on His mind. He had just had an argument with the religious leaders in the temple, and they had picked up stones to kill Him. So He hid Himself and left the temple. John, chapter 9, begins with the words, "As He passed by, He saw..." The blind beggar probably wouldn't have thought twice about it if Jesus had just continued walking by. I'm sure many people passed him each day without stopping. However, Jesus noticed the man's plight, and He had compassion on him, and stopped to help him.

The Father is never too busy or too distracted to notice one person. Your Father sees your need. He is willing to intervene on your behalf and get His hands dirty. He loves you so much that He pays attention to what is going on in your life and in your heart. He wants to listen to your story. He wants to process your emotions with you. He longs to heal you and give you peace. Take your need to Him today. He can handle it.

Further reading: Genesis 16:13, John 1:48

Your Father allows trials so that we may see and display His glory.

Read: John 9:1-12

Everyone was convinced that the ailment of the man born blind was caused by sin, either his own or his parents' sin. Jesus squashed that theory pretty fast when He said, "It was neither that this man sinned, nor his parents; but it was so that the works of God might be displayed in him." Sometimes tough stuff does happen as a result of our sin or another person's sin, but not always. There are trials the Father allows so we will see Him and so others can see His glory in us. He seeks His own glory, not just because He deserves it, but because He knows it's best for us to recognize and acknowledge Him.

Your Father sees every trial you've faced. He knows every pain you've felt, and He has hurt and cried with you. Has He used that trial to draw you closer to Him yet? Has He used your trial to display His glory? If not, He will. He promised! The blind man's trial ended with physical healing. Maybe yours will, too. Or maybe yours will end with the emotional and spiritual healing you don't even realize you need most. Take your trials to your Father. Entrust those hardships to Him, and He will accomplish good things!

Further Reading: Psalm 66:12, Psalm 138:8

Your Father takes care of His children, even on days when everyone else is focused on other things.

Read: John 9:13-14

It was the Sabbath Day, so everyone was focused on going to the temple, obeying the rules, and not doing any work. Jesus noticed a man born blind, and He couldn't help but heal him. Jesus saw the man's great need even when everyone else passed him by or looked down on him because of his infirmity. The Sabbath day had everyone's attention, but Jesus loved the man enough to set aside the rules and responsibilities to meet him at his point of need.

Do you ever find yourself screaming for someone to meet your needs? Do you ever feel weary of being concerned for everybody else when no one seems concerned for you? Your Father sees what you need. He's more than able to take care of you. Spend some time talking with Him today, telling Him how you feel. He will start providing for you right there as you sit in His presence.

Further Reading: Psalm 23:1-6, Matthew 6:25-34

Your Father desires for you to share the truth about Him with others.

Read: John 9:15-23

The blind man knew he was in a precarious position after being healed on the Sabbath. If he claimed Jesus was the Messiah, he would be kicked out of the synagogue. He would be ostracized and rejected. However, sharing the good news about the Messiah was most important, so he just told the truth.

Maybe you have some history that you feel ashamed to share. Your Father wants you to encourage and strengthen others with the story of His faithfulness in your life. The Holy Spirit often uses the stories of God's work in people to draw others to the Father. You are called to share the miracles of grace and forgiveness and healing. Thank your Father today for His goodness, and ask Him how He wants you to share His love through your own testimony.

Further Reading: 2 Corinthians 1:4, Acts 4:18-20, 2 Corinthians 5:18-20

Your Father works miracles no other person in all of history could do!

Read: John 9:24-33

After convincing the religious leaders that he really was born blind, the man who had been healed by Jesus boiled his whole story down to one fact. No one else had ever been able to do what Jesus did. No doctor on earth, no magician or Pharisee, could have restored sight to this blind man, yet Jesus had no problem healing him! I'm sure the man and his parents had given up on healing and gotten comfortable with life like it was. Then Jesus came on the scene and shook things up.

Is there an area of your life where you've given up hope for healing? Have you tried doctors and medicine and therapy and training and support groups? Are you still addicted or hurting or restless? Your Father wants you to know nothing is beyond His power to heal. Nothing physical, psychological, emotional, or spiritual. Even if a thousand other people have tried to help and failed you, your Father gives you hope. Take it to Him, and listen to Him give you your next steps.

Further Reading: Exodus 15:11, Psalm 35:9-10, Psalm 71:19

Your Father seeks out the person who has been burned by religion.

Read: John 9:30-41

When Jesus healed the man who'd been blind from birth, he caused quite a stir in town. The Pharisees and teachers of the Law were furious that Jesus would heal on the Sabbath. So they questioned the man who'd been healed, but still refused to believe. Instead, they threw the man out of the synagogue for testifying about Jesus. When Jesus heard this had happened, He went after the man.

Have you also been burned by people in the church who should have united with you and loved you? Maybe you were fired...judged...criticized...ostracized...forced to leave. The Father knows how it feels to be rejected by people who should love you the most. His heart breaks when His children mistreat one another. Your Father is unlike any other person who walks on this earth. He will never abandon you or shame you. He will pursue you relentlessly because He loves you that much.

Further Reading: Psalm 27:10, Psalm 140:12

Your Father calls you by name and leads you with His own voice.

Read: John 10:1-3

The people to whom Jesus was speaking would have understood the analogy of a shepherd with his sheep very well. Many times in the Old Testament, God's people are compared to sheep. Shepherding was a common occupation in that area of the world. The people would've also known that sheep tend to intermingle peacefully on a hillside with another herd. When it is time to separate them, the shepherd simply calls, and they follow their own shepherd's voice.

Dear One, your Father not only calls to you; He calls you by name. You are not one person in a crowd to Him. Your face does not get lost among all the others that He sees. You matter to Him. Your Father has never forgotten your name or ignored your existence. He sees you where you are and notices all that you do. He loves to be close to you and call you His own.

Further Reading: Psalm 23:1, Isaiah 40:11

Your Father does not lead you where He hasn't already been.

Read: John 10:4-5

A good shepherd walks ahead of the flock, leading them to safe places where there is plenty of food and water. A good shepherd will not just follow the lead of his sheep. The flock needs him to show them where to go and provide for their needs. A good shepherd knows the condition of every lamb in the flock. He pays attention to the details for them. He recognizes each one individually and takes good care of them.

Your Father is not surprised by your situation. He knew way before you did where you were headed. He saw the decisions you and others would make, and He knew all along where you would end up. See, your Father has gone ahead of you. Think of it like a trail guide with a machete, cutting the tall grasses off the path so you can see where you're stepping. Your trail guide will run into all the spider webs stretched across the path before you do. He'll show you where to watch your step for fallen logs or snake holes. He's been this way before. No matter how unique your circumstances seem to be, you're not the only one who's ever walked this road. Your Father has taken this journey with others before you. He knows best how to navigate the treachery of this world's trails. Know that whatever lies before you today, your Father has already been there and scouted out your way. Follow Him closely, and you'll make it to where you're going.

Further Reading: Exodus 33:14-15, Psalm 23:2-4, Psalm 139:5

Your Father is a good Teacher, and He shows you examples to help you understand.

Read: John 10:6-10

Jesus was trying to show the people a picture of the Father, and they weren't understanding. So He drew an analogy to sheep and their shepherd. When you don't understand what your Father is trying to say to you, He will give you examples to help you get it.

I grew up with low self-esteem, and the most pervasive lie the enemy told me was, "You're not worth it." I can look back over my life and see so many times my Father tried to tell me the truth, but I couldn't hear it. Then He sent a step-father named John Jeffrey into my life, and everything he did for me told me I was worth it. He forgave me quickly and lavished his love on me when I didn't deserve it. He showed me more than anyone else on earth what the Father of *this* prodigal was really like. My Father sent someone to show me the truth because I couldn't conceive it.

Maybe you're like me, struggling to receive the truth from your Father because the lies are so loud in your head. Maybe that's why you're holding this book in your hand. Maybe He's using analogy after analogy from Jesus' life to show you who He really is so you can learn to trust Him.

Further Reading: Luke 15:1-32

Your Father is committed to His own and fights for them no matter what.

Read: John 10:11-18

Jesus described His commitment to His own by declaring that He would lay down His very life, just as a good shepherd would do for his sheep. He also declared His desire to shepherd not just the Jews, but all people. His love for us extends beyond the boundaries of race, religion, creed, and tradition. He desires for us all to call Him Father and live life as His dear children.

The Father fought for us by sending Jesus to become the sacrifice we could not provide for ourselves. Jesus was the only perfect Lamb able to save us from our sins so we can spend eternity with our Father. Even though it cost Him the life of His Son, our Father believes we are worth it. He will stop at nothing to save us and draw us to Himself. He will move heaven and earth for you to see Him and know Him and trust Him. Walk closely with your Father today, and know that there is nothing more important to Him than you, His precious child.

Further Reading: Zephaniah 3:17, Psalm 121:5-8, 2 Thessalonians 3:3

Your Father cannot be completely comprehended.

Read: John 10:19-21

The Jews were expecting a Messiah much more militaristic than Jesus. They struggled to reconcile their expectations with the miracles He was performing and the dynamic teaching He offered. I've heard it said, "Hindsight is 20/20." I suppose in this instance that's true. So many people in Biblical times didn't understand when Jesus was fulfilling the prophecies of the Messiah. Many people today are still confused, but even if we understand the gospel, there's a lot about our Father we'll never comprehend until we get to Heaven.

Take comfort in the fact that your Father doesn't fit into a little box with a nice, neat bow on top. If He was that simple, could He really handle all the problems of this world? Your Father is as complex as He is wonderful. He can be studied every day for the rest of your life, and you will barely scratch the surface of His amazing character. Stay the course, and get to know Him as much as you can. You have no higher calling in life.

Further Reading: Job 11:7-9, Romans 11:33-36

Your Father is greater, stronger, and more powerful than all others.

Read: John 10:22-29

Jesus continued revealing the Father to the Jewish leaders and proving by His miracles that He was the Messiah. Still, so many would not believe. They persecuted the ones who did believe. They threw them out of the synagogues and refused to eat with them. They rejected anyone who did not reject Jesus. Later, after Jesus' resurrection and ascension, some followers were even killed for their faith.

People can do a lot of evil in this world if God allows it. But never forget this: your Father is able to keep you in His hand. No one can snatch you away from Him, no matter what they do to you. No matter how much you have been persecuted, abused, ridiculed, or ostracized, your Father keeps you in His hand. He will never let you go.

Further Reading: Psalm 16:8, Psalm 94:18, Zechariah 2:8

Your Father's works are GOOD.

Read: John 10:30-42

The religious leaders could not stand Jesus. He broke the mold everyday of what they thought a "godly" person should look like. They tried again and again to trap Him into saying or doing something wrong so they could accuse Him, but it never worked! Not once did Jesus give them reason to believe He was not from the Father. Never once did He lose control or give in to the pressure of who the people wanted Him to be. He was true to His mission, and all His works were good.

Your Father has never said or done anything against His own character. He is GOOD – all the time. In fact, such goodness flows from His heart toward His children that He would do anything for you. He lavishes love on you, *especially* when you don't deserve it. He wants only the best for you. He desperately desires to bless you, most of all with His presence and counsel. I've said it before, and I'll say it again: your Father proves Himself to you by His works. He can be trusted.

Further Reading: Psalm 145:8-10, Ephesians 2:10

Your Father always has a plan.

Read: John 11:1-6

It was no accident that Jesus stayed where He was for two days after He received the news of Lazarus' illness. He knew Lazarus would die, and He had plans to raise him back to life. I wonder if Jesus had shown up earlier, if Mary and Martha would have begged Him so hard to heal their brother that He would have had a hard time saying no. He loved them so much, and it hurt Him to see them hurt. In fact, He even wept with them (John 11:35). So why wait? Jesus intentionally arranged the details to accomplish the Father's plan and give Him glory.

Your Father is very purposeful with the timing and events in your life. He is weaving a beautiful tapestry through your story. Wait for Him. Trust Him. Seek out His plan because His way really is best. He knows what He is doing.

Further Reading: Psalm 27:14, Psalm 37:4-6, John 6:5-6

Your Father is not discouraged by danger.

Read: John 11:7-10

Jesus' disciples were concerned when Jesus decided to go back to Judea. The last time they were there, the Jewish leaders had wanted to stone Him to death! However, God had a plan, and nothing was going to deter Jesus from accomplishing it. He was going to go to Bethany to see His friends, Mary and Martha, and take care of their brother, Lazarus.

Are you reassured, Dear One, to know that Your Father isn't afraid? He is so powerful that evil doesn't scare Him a bit. Since we're with Him, evil need not scare us, either. He knows what is to come, and He has a plan before you even realize a plan is needed. Stick with your Father, Beloved. He can handle anything that comes your way.

Further Reading: Psalm 27:1, Psalm 56:3-4, Psalm 118:6

Your Father meets you in hard places.

Read: John 11:11-15

I wonder if the disciples were surprised when Jesus told them Lazarus had died and He was glad He wasn't there. I would've been. Unlike His disciples, Jesus knew of the great victory that was ahead and the people who would believe in Him after He raised Lazarus from the dead. Jesus understood that the hardest times in life soften our hearts towards Him.

Your Father is especially near to you when life feels unbearable. He draws you extra close when you feel most desperate. Think about the hardest times in your life, the seasons when you realized what is most important and what really has no long term significance. Tragedy and loss tend to expand our vision beyond the little things that irritate us and force us to seek comfort. Would you ever experience the comfort of Your Father if you could make it without Him? Would you accept His free gift of salvation if you didn't know you needed it? Your Father uses the storms of life to draw you into His warm embrace. Enjoy His arms around you today.

Further Reading: Psalm 34:18, Psalm 119:71-72, Romans 8:20-21

Your Father's presence changes everything!

Read: John 11:15-21

Martha ran to Jesus when He finally arrived because her brother, Lazarus, had died. She had sent word to Jesus days before that he was sick and needed healing, but Jesus didn't come right away. When Martha asked Jesus to come, she knew He could heal Lazarus. She also knew if He was there, everything would be okay. The whole world could be at his bedside, but if Jesus wasn't there, the situation would not change. Martha knew that Jesus' presence would change everything.

Is there an area of your life that needs healing? Restoration? Transformation? Have you tried self-help books, or support groups, or meditation? Are you feeling hopeless that your situation could ever improve? Remember, the Father's presence changes everything! He longs for you to invite Him into the mess and pain. He longs to do for you what He does best. His intervention and provision are always what you need most. Ask your Father for His presence in your deepest need, and He will make all the difference in the world.

Further study: Exodus 33:15, Hebrews 13:5

Your Father is never forceful.

Read: John 11:20-26

Martha was so disappointed Jesus hadn't come to heal her brother when she first called for Him, and, in true Martha fashion, she wasn't shy about telling Him so. Jesus' response to her grief is a hard truth to swallow, especially when a loved one has just passed away. Jesus said to her, "Everyone who lives and believes in Me will never die." Then He asked an interesting question: "Do you believe this?" Jesus gave Martha the option to believe Him or not.

I've heard it said that God is a gentleman. I'll be honest. I haven't known very many true gentlemen in my lifetime, and it comforts me to know my Father never forces Himself on anyone. We're drawn to Him because of His love and grace, not by threats or intimidation. Your Father isn't offended when you struggle to believe Him. He desperately wants you to believe because He knows it changes everything, but He won't punish you for having doubts. He lavished His love on you to draw you to Himself. Wrestle with that question today: "Do you believe?"

Further Reading: 1 John 4:18-19, Acts 16:31

Your Father is never in a rush.

Read: John 11:26-30

When Martha met Jesus, He was still outside the village. She called Mary to Him, and He waited. He wasn't in a hurry to get to Lazarus' tomb and work a miracle. It was most important to Him to stop and listen to His friends. He wanted Martha and Mary to feel heard and comforted. They were not merely interrupting His journey; He gave Himself fully to them in the moment.

Have you ever had someone ask, "How are you?" as they walk past you in the hallway? They don't stop to listen. They don't really want an answer to the question because they're on their way to something they feel is urgent. Your Father is never too hurried to stop and listen to you. You're never an interruption or an inconvenience to Him. He loves you dearly and wants to have conversation with you. Hear Him ask, "How are you?" and then tell Him honestly how you are doing. He will give you all the time you need.

Further Reading: Matthew 20:30-34, 2 Peter 3:8

Your Father cares for you so deeply that He is moved by your emotions.

Read: John 11:31-38

After Lazarus, the brother of Mary and Martha, died, his sisters were distraught. They didn't understand why Jesus hadn't come quickly when they called for Him. They each had a mixed up ball of emotions that they handed Jesus when He arrived. Anger, frustration, grief, exhaustion, pain...But Jesus was able to handle all their feelings. In fact, John 11:33 and 38 tell us Jesus was "deeply moved" when He saw those He loved weeping, and He wept with them. Even though He planned to heal Lazarus, He shared the broken hearts of those He loved.

Your Father cares so deeply for you. He weeps when you weep. He hurts when you hurt. His love for you is so deep that your feelings have a profound effect on His. What makes you sad? Why are you grieving? Your Father cares, and He is ready to wrap His arms around you and comfort you. The psalmist says the Father catches our tears in a bottle (Psalm 56:8). In other words, not one tear is forgotten or overlooked by Him. Our human minds cannot even comprehend the depths of His great love for us. He is for you, my friend. Pour out your feelings to Him. Let Him cry with you and comfort you. He cares more than you can imagine.

Further Study: Psalm 103:13, Psalm 138:3

Your Father's voice is powerful.

Read: John 11:38-44

When Jesus went to Lazarus' tomb, he had been dead for four days, yet Jesus spoke life into him. He didn't have to reach out and touch Lazarus as He did when He healed a leper. He didn't have to make mud and put it on him as He had done for a blind man. He simply spoke the words, "Lazarus, come forth!" and the miracle was done.

When my son was only five years old, I got pregnant, and no one was more excited than he was. He helped name the baby and talked about her all the time. When we had an ultrasound that told us her heart had stopped beating, we prayed for two weeks that God would give her back to us. My son told me, "Jesus told Lazarus' heart to start beating again and it did! He can do that for our baby, too!" But despite all our begging, our Father did not give us the miracle we hoped for. I remember telling my son, "Just because He *didn't* heal on this earth doesn't mean He *couldn't* heal." We chose to trust Him.

Your Father's voice is so powerful He can speak a miracle into your life at any moment. Where do you need some divine intervention? Ask Him for it. He may not answer the way you want Him to, but that doesn't mean He can't. Your Father is wise in His decisions, and He sees the big picture we can't see. We may not understand until we get to Heaven why He did what He did, but we can rest assured His motive is always love. He is a good, good Father.

Further Reading: Genesis 1:3, Isaiah 55:11, Matthew 8:8 and 13

Your Father can accomplish His will, even through people who don't believe Him.

Read: John 11:45-53

After Jesus raised Lazarus from the dead, so many people believed in Him that the Jewish religious leaders were afraid they would lose their following and social status. The high priest, Caiaphas, suggested it would be better for Jesus to die than for Him to lead the whole Jewish nation astray. John points out he wasn't speaking his own mind when he said this. God had already determined how Jesus would become the sacrifice to save people from their sins. So He moved Caiaphas to suggest His divine plan without even realizing it.

Your Father is all-powerful, all-knowing, and all-wise. You don't have to worry that you'll ruin His plan. No matter what you've done or what's been done to you, your Father's desires are not devastated. If you have a willing heart, He can work it out no matter what. It is not your responsibility, Dear One, to figure out your Father's plan and make it happen. That's more weight than your shoulders can bear. Your job is simply to listen and obey…one day at a time. Your Father will handle the rest.

Further Reading: Psalm 37:23, Proverbs 16:9, Romans 11:29

Your Father is discerning.

Read: John 11:53-57

When the religious leaders began plotting how they would kill Jesus, He didn't go face them head on – not just yet. He was wise and discerning in His timing – both in words and actions. He didn't go start an argument with the Jewish teachers or accuse them of evil. He didn't gather up a crowd of people to defend Him and start a riot. Instead, Jesus took His disciples and stayed in a city called Ephraim near the wilderness. He waited there for His Father to reveal the right timing and the right direction.

Your Father sees the big picture that you can't see. We've talked about this before, but it bears repeating. Your Father knows the best timing and the best direction for you to go, and His counsel can be trusted. What area of your life necessitates divine wisdom today? Ask Your Father for it and then listen for Him to answer. He promises to deliver.

Further Reading: James 1:5, Romans 12:2, 1 John 4:1-3

Your Father is relational.

Read: John 12:1-2

Jesus had large crowds seeking and following Him. Knowing what a short time He had on this earth, I struggle to imagine Him just sitting down with friends for a relaxing meal, but that's exactly what He did. He didn't work miracles until He dropped and sleep a few hours and do it all over again. He didn't eat on the run so He could accomplish more. Jesus was so relational. That's one of the reasons so many people wanted to be around Him.

Your Father is relational. He loves spending time with His children. He prioritizes slowing down and sharing life with you. Your Father wants to help you slow down enough to spend some extra time with Him. Life is busy, but nothing is more important than spending time with your Father. He lavishes His love on you. He prepares you for what is ahead. He wants to hear what you are thinking and talk with you about what's on His mind. He cares for you more than you can imagine.

Further Reading: Matthew 9:36, Matthew 19:14

Your Father deserves extravagant sacrifice.

Read: John 12:1-8

During the meal Jesus was sharing with friends at Lazarus' house, Mary poured a bottle of perfume that cost a year's wages onto Jesus' feet. She also let down her hair, something a woman in that culture did not do in public. Mary sacrificed her most valuable possession and her reputation for Jesus. She loved Him extravagantly in front of all the dinner guests. Jesus had changed everything for her, and that made her love Him lavishly.

Have you begun to experience the incredible transformation that results when you receive the deep love of your Father? Have you decided yet that He is worthy of your most valuable possession? Have you truly surrendered every single part of your life, your body, your relationships, and your schedule to Him? Consider for a moment if you really believe He is worth it. If you aren't there yet, be honest with your Father. He would love to process those feelings with you. If you are so much in awe of His love and grace that you want to give Him everything, then tell Him! Sacrifice for Him! Love your Father by the way you live your life today.

Further Reading: Psalm 40:5-10, Hosea 6:6

Your Father ALWAYS keeps His word.

Read: John 12:12-16

Over three hundred prophecies were written about Jesus in the Old Testament hundreds and thousands of years before He was born. Hear this: He fulfilled every single one. Despite this, John wrote in chapter 12, verse 16 that the disciples didn't understand at first, and he wasn't kidding! Only after Jesus' death and resurrection did it all began to make sense, and they realized the Father NEVER breaks a promise.

Have you ever had someone break a promise to you? We all know how it feels to be betrayed. Believe it or not, your Father knows what that feels like too (see John 18:2). You can depend on Him to be faithful to His word. Never — not one single time — has He ever broken a promise. He loves you and will always come through for you.

Further Reading: 2 Timothy 2:13, Joshua 23:14, Isaiah 55:11

Your Father gave hope when He conquered death.

Read: John 12:17-19

When Jesus called Lazarus out of the tomb that had been his resting place for four days, news travelled fast! Everyone was talking about the miracle of Lazarus' resurrection. His situation had seemed so tragic and so hopeless before the miracle. (Dear One, have I told you lately that no situation is hopeless with our God?) Hope filled the surrounding towns and villages when the people heard of the man who could raise the dead. The people who saw such a miracle couldn't keep from talking about it!

What area of your life could use a resurrection? Your marriage? Your identity? Your finances? Your relationships? Listen closely to me, my dear. There is absolutely no situation that is beyond a miracle from your Father. He sees you and loves you, and He is intervening on your behalf. If He can raise the dead, surely there is nothing He cannot do! Trust in His miracle-working power.

Further reading: 1 Corinthians 15:54-55, Hebrews 11:17-19, Revelation 21:4

Your Father is not sidetracked or indecisive.

Read: John 12:20-23

Greeks and Romans and Jews were all together in Jerusalem at the time of the Passover feast. Many people were asking Jesus' disciples if they could see Jesus. When Andrew and Philip came to tell Jesus, He said to them, "The hour has come for the Son of Man to be glorified." He had His mind on the mission – the Father's rescue mission. All the people that flocked to Jesus wanted to see Him perform miracles, but He was determined to accomplish what He was sent to do.

Your Father is not sidetracked by the choices you or other people have made. He doesn't randomly change His mind or decide Plan B would be better. Your Father is on a mission. He wants to spend time with you so He can transform you to look more like Him. He wants to reveal Himself to you and through you to others. He will continue working on His plan for your life. You can trust Him to bring it to pass.

Further Reading: Psalm 138:8, Romans 8:20-21, 2 Corinthians 3:18

Your Father is willing to sacrifice everything – even His very life – for you.

Read: John 12:24-27

Jesus had told His disciples plainly that He would be killed and then raised back to life on the third day. As the time drew nearer, Jesus knew He would soon endure the most barbaric, tortuous death possible. His soul was troubled (vs. 27), but He kept His eye on the prize – you! He refused to ask the Father to save Him from painful torture and death because He knew this act would serve the very purpose for which He came to earth.

Did you know the Father had you on His mind when He sent Jesus to the cross? You were "the joy set before Him" (Hebrews 12:2) that allowed Him to accomplish the mission. Your Father would do anything for you. He moves Heaven and Earth to take care of you. He goes to the ends of the earth to prove His love for you. No matter what it costs Him, you are worth it. Bask in the love of your Father today.

Further Reading: John 3:16-17, Philippians 2:5-8

Your Father's voice is deep and soothing like thunder.

Read: John 12:27-32

Have you ever curled up on a fluffy couch with a good book in a thunderstorm? Gentle thunder rumbles outside. Rain pitter-patters lightly on the windows. The daylight is dim, and you feel so cozy. When God the Father spoke audibly to Jesus, no one was afraid. It didn't make anyone tremble or run and hide. His voice was so deep and soothing that some people thought it had thundered. Others thought maybe an angel had spoken.

How do you imagine the tone of your Father when He speaks to you? Do you assume His tone is full of anger and judgment? Disappointment? How about love and gentleness? Kindness? The truth is your Father yearns to speak kindly to you. He longs to calm your fears with His voice. The next time you hear the deep rumble of distant thunder, consider what the soothing voice of your Father is saying to you.

Further Study: Romans 2:4, John 5:25, Revelation 3:20

Your Father offers to everyone the invitation to become His child and spread His light.

Read: John 12:32-36

Jesus was speaking to a whole crowd of people when He prophesied the death He was going to die. He invited all of them – Jews, Gentiles, religious leaders, people from every walk of life – to believe in Him and become "children of the Light." It didn't matter what their family tree looked like or what they had accomplished with their lives. Jesus called out to the whole crowd, bidding all to come to Him. This is the same message He spoke to Nicodemus: "God so loved the world that He gave His one and only Son, that *whoever* believes in Him will not perish, but have eternal life" (John 3:16, italics mine).

Your family tree doesn't disqualify you from being a child of the Light. Your past actions, your present situation, and your future decisions don't change the Father's invitation. When you become a child of God, you will begin to look like your Father and spread His light in the world around you. Which of your characteristics resemble His? Which ones don't remind you of Him at all? If you don't see the resemblance yet, don't get discouraged. Wait for Him to give you direction. The longer you walk with Him, the more you will look like Him. Be patient, dear child, and remember He's not done with you yet.

Further Reading: 1 John 3:1, 1 John 3:10, 1 John 3:18

Your Father is very convincing!

Read: John 12:37-43

Despite all the heavenly signs they saw, some people still refused to believe in Jesus. The Father knew this would be the case, so He prompted Isaiah to prophecy about it several hundred years before Jesus was even born. However, Jesus was so convincing by His miracles, by His compassion, and by His wisdom, that even some of the religious leaders believed Him. The more they knew Him, the more they trusted Him.

If you walk with your Father long enough, you will experience His faithfulness again and again. He will prove Himself to you by His actions and through the Holy Spirit. Have you asked Him to show you His footprints in your story? Can you see how He has been involved all along? Your Father never makes a mistake, never messes up. He can always be trusted. The more you spend time with Him, the more you will know Him. Remember, Dear One, to know Him is to trust Him!

Further Reading: John 2:23, John 7:31, Psalm 28:7

Your Father wants you free from darkness – now and for eternity.

Read: John 12:44-50

You and I don't have to look very far to find suffering and injustice all around us. Jesus lived in a world much like ours, overflowing with hatred and violence, murder and stealing and lying, selfishness and pride. All of this darkness threatens to overwhelm us and make us slaves to our own wicked appetites. We can easily fall prey to worry and fear. Drugs, alcohol, and pornography promise relief for us, but leave us addicted instead. Jesus wanted people to be free from the darkness that rules on this earth, prepared for eternity with the Father, and separated from evil forever.

Your Father desires freedom for you. He loves you so much that He sent Jesus so you could know Him and be released from the power of sin. Believing the truth about your Father and acting on it is the way to be free. He gave His commandments to show you the best way to live this life and prepare for eternity. That is what He wants most for you. He sacrificed everything so you could be His child forever.

Further Reading: 1 John 1:5-7, 1 John 2:28

Your Father's right view of Himself allows Him to serve selflessly.

Read: John 13:1-5

The evening before He went to the cross, Jesus met with His friends for one last Passover meal. When they arrived, there was no servant there to wash their feet, which were dirty from walking the dusty streets of Jerusalem. Washing feet was considered the lowest job for the lowest servant in the house, but Jesus knew who He was. He knew the mission He had been given. With that in mind, He took on the most menial task, the lowest job, and served His disciples in a way they would never forget.

Do you know who you are? More importantly, do you know *Whose* you are? Your perfect Father actually serves you! He loves to serve you! Let that sink in a moment. Then, when you know how your Father lavishes His love on you, and when you know how selflessly He serves you, you will be able to serve others in the same way.

Further study: Philippians 2:3-8, Mark 10:43-45

Your Father serves people who don't understand — even His enemies.

Read John 13:5-12

Do you know someone you think deserves to be served? Someone who pours herself out day after day and could use a break? This is not how Jesus chooses who He will serve. Do you realize He even washed the feet of Judas, the one He knew would betray Him to His death that very night? He cradled each filthy foot in His hands – hands that would soon be driven through with nails. He tenderly wiped the dirt and grime away until each of His disciples – including Judas, the Betrayer – had feet clean enough for reclining at the table.

No matter what your life looks like, no matter how messy you've gotten, no matter if you have betrayed your Father and spit in His face, He desires to lavish His love on you. He takes care of you even when He receives no thanks. He can't help but provide for you because He loves you that much. Bring Him your mess so He can start cleaning you up. Bask in His love, and feel the tender touch of your Father today.

Further Reading: Romans 5:8, Romans 8:32-39

Your Father is all-knowing.

Read: John 13:10-11

Jesus set a beautiful example for His disciples, not just in serving, but in forgiving and loving too. Judas may have fooled everyone else, but Jesus saw his heart and discerned his motives. I can't imagine how difficult it must have been for Judas to allow Jesus to wash his feet, considering what he was about to do. I wonder if he even understood that Jesus was calling him out specifically when He said, "Not all of you are clean."

If you have been hurt by someone who has pulled the wool over everyone else's eyes, your Father knows. If you have pretended to be someone you are not, even if everyone else has believed you, your Father knows the real you. Your heart, your emotions, and your motives are all understood by your faithful Father. Even if you don't know why you are the way you are, He knows. He sees everything about you and loves you more than anyone else ever will.

Further Reading: Isaiah 11:2-3, Matthew 9:4, Mark 2:8, Romans 11:33

Your Father so loves His children that He considers loving them the best way to show our love for Him.

Read: John 13:12-17

When Jesus knew His time on earth was coming to an end, He gave His disciples a striking picture of the service He intended for them to continue. Gathering with the Twelve for the Passover meal, Jesus performed the job reserved for the lowest servant in the house. After He washed the feet of the disciples, He instructed them to serve one another as He had served them. Then He continued to demonstrate His sacrificial love by going to the cross and laying down His very life for them.

Your Father loves you so much that He has asked people to serve you. When people serve you, His child, He considers that a service to Himself (John 13:20). If you have a child or a pet, consider what it would feel like for someone else to step in and love that child or pet if you couldn't. As a foster parent, I have often talked with the Father about a child we have taken into our home, knowing that our child belongs to Him. We love them like our own because He loves them that much. Your Father wants you to feel His love, so He sends people your way to be His hands and feet. Then, when you receive His love lavished on you, you can pour out His love to others.

Further Reading: Romans 12:10, Galatians 5:13, 1 John 4:19

Your Father wants to help you believe.

Read: John 13:18-20

Jesus told His disciples many events before they came to be with the intention of helping them believe (vs. 19). He didn't ask them to follow Him blindly. He understood the fragility of their faith, so He anticipated what signs would leave them utterly convinced He was the Messiah. Their faith in Jesus would need to be strong, as these men would eventually lose their lives for what they believed about Him.

Your Father understands when your faith is weak. He doesn't chide you for not believing every word He has said. He's happy to earn your trust. He knows why you struggle to believe, even if you don't know why. Moreover, your Father knows what you need to see or hear or understand in order to believe Him. Maybe that's why you are holding this book in your hand right now. Your Father has sent these truths your way because He wants to help you believe who He really is. Give Him a chance to earn your trust. You will never be disappointed you did.

Further Reading: Mark 9:24, John 6:29, John 12:30

Your Father uses the evil intentions of man to further His cause.

Read: John 13:21-30

Can you imagine if Jesus had taken away Judas' free choice to betray Him? Then Jesus wouldn't have ended up in custody of the religious leaders. Ultimately, Judas' betrayal led Jesus to the cross, but if He didn't die on the cross, there would be no perfect sacrifice to cover our sins and allow us to come to the Father. I am so grateful God chose to use even Judas' sin to accomplish His rescue plan.

I've heard it said that many people would not come to the Father if it weren't for the hard things in life. If we could erase the sins of one person against another, we would erase the very thing that God often uses to draw them to Himself. I've endured plenty of hardship in my own life, and I see my Father using that for His glory. It amazes me how He does that, but He does! Even sin cannot thwart God's perfect plan.

Further Reading: Genesis 50:20, Romans 8:28

Your Father lets you – even wants you – in His personal space.

Read: John 13:23-25

Passover tradition places the youngest person present to the right of the leader of the Passover meal. That's why John was next to Jesus at the last supper. When Jesus told His disciples that one of them would betray Him, everyone wanted to know who. John was the closest one to Jesus, so He leaned back on Jesus' chest to ask Him the question. Jesus didn't chide him for getting in His personal space. He responded as if John had been this close to Him on many occasions before. Likely, he had.

Your Father doesn't want to keep you at arm's length. He wants you to be comfortable in His embrace. He invites you to lean your head on His chest and ask your heart's deepest questions. It takes a lot of trust to get in someone's personal space. Your Father is completely trustworthy. He bids you come as close to Him as you like because He loves you more than you can imagine. His space is your space because that's the kind of Father He is.

Further Reading: Mark 10:16, Luke 7:37-39, James 4:8

Your Father cares more about being glorified than about personal comfort.

Read: John 13:31-33

When Judas left the Passover meal, Jesus knew the time was drawing near when He would accomplish the greatest act of love in all of history. His eyes weren't on the praise He would one day receive. He was looking to you and me, ready to do anything to save us. The original Greek word for "glorified" in verse 32 means "to magnify, to make renowned." Jesus knew that being glorified would reveal His Father's character to people for the rest of time. He so desperately wanted people to know the Father that He set aside all personal comfort to reveal Him.

Your Father knows that when you see Him glorified, you will know how much He loves you. He knows that when you believe in the sacrifice He made for you, you will want to draw near to Him. He knows that His glory is what is best for you and every other person on this earth. Today, as in Biblical times, He faithfully continues to reveal Himself to His children. How has He been drawing you close lately? How has He been showing His character to you – and through you – recently? Set your mind on your Father today, and share His love with others.

Further Reading: Psalm 86:12, Isaiah 43:19-21, Matthew 5:16

Your Father's love is what sets Him apart from all others.

John 13:34-35

Some people are known by their job title. Some are known by something terrible they did, or a success they achieved. Some are even known for a phrase they've said or their appearance. Jesus told His disciples the way the world would know they belonged to Him was by their love. That's why He told them to serve others as He had served them. By serving, they demonstrated His love.

Your Father is known for a lot of reasons. He's known for creating the world, for sending a worldwide flood, for parting the Red Sea. Perhaps He is best known for sending His Son to become the sacrifice that would save all His children from their sins. Your Father is most famous for His love. He cares so deeply for you that He intervenes on your behalf. His love isn't like any other person's affection. He loves you more. He loves you better. His love is what sets Him apart from all others.

Further Reading: Romans 5:8, Romans 8:38-39

Your Father understands, so you don't have to.

Read: John 13:36-38

When Peter asked Jesus where He was going, Jesus didn't answer the question directly. He basically told Peter, "I know where I am going, and I will make sure you join Me there later. You'll just have to trust Me." When Peter protested that they should not be separated, Jesus pointed out that he would deny even knowing Him three times that night. Peter did not understand at all, but Jesus did.

You may have personal experiences laying heavy on your heart that you don't understand. Child abuse, tragic loss, mental illness, miscarriages, failed adoptions, frail health. We don't understand these things, but we can be comforted that our Father does. Can we really trust that He knows what He's doing? Absolutely, we can! He sees the big picture. He knows the ripple effects of every single action and inaction He allows. He is the Master at working it all out for our good and for His glory. I've experienced it many times, and you will, too, if you just trust Him.

Further Reading: Psalm 139:12, Isaiah 40:28, Romans 8:28

Your Father wants you to live with Him, and He has a special place in mind for you.

Read: John 14:1-3

My husband and I have been remodeling our bathroom for the last few weeks. We found rotten wood in the floor when we pulled up the old tiles, so we replaced the floor. Then we fixed the walls and painted, and that's when we realized the vanity, mirror, and light fixtures were completely outdated. So we switched out those, too. When we got close to being finished, we saw how warm and inviting the whole room looked, and wanted to run with the feeling it created. We bought a shelf and added a picture and an inspirational plaque. Finally, we added an air freshener to complete our cozy space.

Your Father knows what is cozy and inviting to you. He knows what you like and what you don't. He has a place in His house tailor-made just for you, His child. He doesn't have to fix rotten floor boards or replace fixtures that are out of date. And your room won't be given to anyone else in the meantime. He has prepared it just for you because He loves you. Your Father has you on His heart and mind all the time. He is never NOT thinking about you! Sweet child, rest today in the promise you have a special place, prepared just for you.

Further reading: Psalm 27:4, Psalm 139:17

Your Father always tells you the truth.

Read: John 14:4-6

The disciples were still so confused when Jesus told them He was going to leave. Nevertheless, He continued explaining so they would understand later. Even though the truth was hard to hear and even harder to understand, Jesus told His disciples the truth they needed to know. In John 14:6, He told them, "No one comes to the Father but through Me." Historically, this truth has been debated, criticized, quoted, and believed, but it has never changed.

Your Father will always tell you the truth. He will never lead you to believe something that is false. Even though you may not understand, even though it may not be popular, even though it may be hard to swallow, your Father will always be honest with you. People's beliefs will never change who He is or what is true. Your Father can be trusted to know the truth, understand the truth, and speak the truth… no matter what.

Further Reading: Psalm 43:3, John 8:32, Hebrews 6:18

Your Father is sufficient to meet all your needs.

Read: John 14:7-10

Jesus told His disciples again that He was revealing the Father to them, and Philip asked, "Lord, show us the Father, and it is enough for us." The disciples longed to see and know God the Father. They understood that knowing Him is our highest calling. However, they didn't yet understand that Jesus was the exact representation of the Father (Hebrews 1:3). Philip used a Greek word in his request that displays how important it was for him to see and know the Father. The original word for "it is enough" is *arkeo*, and can also be translated "sufficient, possessed of unfailing strength, content." In other words, Philip was pointing out that no need of his was greater than knowing the Father because only the Father could meet all his other needs.

Your Father is sufficient to meet all your needs, too. In fact, He is called *El Shaddai*, which means "God Almighty," also sometimes translated "All-Sufficient One" (Genesis 17:1). No matter how you may feel at this moment, knowing your Father is your greatest need. Your Father put a hunger in your heart that cannot be satisfied by anything or anyone other than Himself, and when you do find your satisfaction in Him, you will be completely content. That's what He wants for you. Take each of your needs and desires to your Father today. Dear child, praise Him for being sufficient for you.

Further Reading: 2 Corinthians 12:9, Philippians 4:11-13, Romans 8:22-25

Your Father wants you to trust Him enough to ask for good gifts.

Read: John 14:11-14

Jesus promised His followers they would do even greater works than His own after He returned to the Father. He clarified *how* they would do all these great things when He told them, "Whatever you ask in My name, that I will do." Asking in Jesus' name means asking according to His will and character. The disciples had been walking with Jesus for three years and knew the kinds of works He did. They'd seen His motives and His priorities again and again. They knew He loved to meet needs and give good gifts to people. They didn't always understand His will perfectly, and their prayers were sometimes answered with a "no," but they trusted Him enough to ask for miracles.

When my three year old asked me to give her a real live pony for her birthday, she made my heart smile. Even though I couldn't give my sweet girl a pony, I could see she trusted my love and commitment to her. That's why she was able to ask for such an extravagant gift. The more you know your Father, the more you will trust Him. Even if His answer is no, He will be so pleased by your faith. Even His "no" may be the good gift you desire. Commit to spending time with your Father every day so you may know Him and trust Him more and more.

Further Reading: Psalm 37:4, Luke 22:42, James 1:17

Your Father wants your love and trust to lead to obedience.

Read: John 14:15

Many of us live life in a cycle of making our own decisions, doing things our own way, finding out our way doesn't work so well, and then blaming God that our life is a mess. When I decided to take my Father at His Word and obey Him, I started experiencing a new cycle. I choose to obey even though I don't understand, and God shows His faithfulness. Then I trust Him more, and obeying the next time is easier. Every time I obey and He proves His faithfulness, my love for Him grows and I trust Him more.

If you are struggling to trust your Father, I challenge you to try obeying Him. He will be faithful to you. He will meet every need and give you peace like you have never experienced before. Remember, love is an action, not just a feeling. Maybe you don't feel love for your Father yet, but you can choose to love Him by obeying Him. When He comes through for you again and again, you will love Him more and trust Him more. Then obeying Him will be easier. He will never let you down.

Further Reading: Deuteronomy 6:24, Isaiah 48:17-18, Psalm 119:165

Your Father never meant for anyone to be fatherless.

Read: John 14:16-18

Fatherlessness is a pandemic in this day and age. Many fathers across the world have died from disease and war. Some are absent. Others are abusive. Fathers are supposed to teach their children, protect them, provide for them, take pride in them. The Father designed us on purpose as children in need of our fathers. This is why, when He was preparing to leave this earth, Jesus said, "I will not leave you as orphans."

If you're like me, it doesn't feel good to need a father. You may want to be self-sufficient so you can't be hurt anymore. You may want to run from anyone who bears that title because your experience with fathers has been terrible. Your Father in Heaven understands your angst. He knows why you feel fearful, angry, defensive, frustrated… He hurts with you when the mere mention of "Father" makes you cringe. In fact, He knows your heart even better than you do. He will prove Himself to you and gently lead you to trust Him. He is willing for you to take your time to learn who He really is. He understands you have to know Him in order to trust Him.

Further Reading: Deuteronomy 31:8, Psalm 27:10, Isaiah 49:15-16

Your Father wants you to "know" Him.

Read: John 14:19-20

Jesus was in the upper room, sharing His very last meal with the disciples when He said, "In that day, you will know that I am in My Father, and you in Me, and I in you." They'd been walking with Him and doing full time ministry with Him for three years! Didn't they know Him already? However, Jesus was about to make the greatest demonstration of His love, His identity, and His mission. The original Greek word for "know" is *ginosko*, which can also be translated "to feel, understand, be resolved, or be sure." Jesus didn't just want His followers to have a lot of head knowledge. He wanted them to know from intimate experience who He really was.

Your Father wants you to experience His love in such a way that you are sure about Him. He wants you to *feel* His love. He desires for your heart to be so resolved about the truth that no one could convince you otherwise. Have you truly experienced the love of your Father? If you know about His love but you struggle to feel it, ask Him to move your knowledge of Him from your head to your heart.

Further Reading: Job 42:5, Jeremiah 24:7, Ephesians 1:18-19

Your Father wants you to love Him with the same love He has loved you.

Read: John 14:21-24

Jesus used the Greek word for love, *agapeo* when He told His disciples, "Whoever has My commands and keeps them is the one who loves Me..." The word *agapeo* is not used for brotherly love or romantic love. It means to love unconditionally. In other words, Jesus chose to love His followers no matter how they let Him down or sinned against Him. He loved them no matter what. Furthermore, He told them their unconditional love for Him would result in obedience.

Many people will cite their reason for disobeying God is something He did or didn't do for them. This isn't the kind of contractual love your Father desires from you. When you truly know Him, you will love and trust Him unconditionally, and your love and trust will lead you to obey Him. Your Father lavishes His love on you, dear Child, no matter what you have done to Him. He chooses to call you His own day after day. He will never stop loving you. Can you commit today to loving Him back no matter what?

Further Reading: Matthew 22:37, John 3:16, 1 John 4:19

Your Father will help you remember what He has told you when you need it.

Read: John 14:25-27

Jesus reminded His disciples that the Holy Spirit would come and dwell with them when He left. He assured them that the Spirit would remind them of what He'd said when they needed it. It wasn't their responsibility to study hard enough to remember every single teaching of Jesus. They didn't have the pressure of knowing what to say when the time came for them to speak. Jesus also told them the Holy Spirit would give them peace – peace that is not like anything this world offers.

Does it bring you peace to know the weight is not on your shoulders to say the right thing all the time and always know the right thing to do? Does it comfort you to be reminded that you have the Holy Spirit with you each moment to guide you and show you the path to take? His Spirit is the best gift the Father has given to His children. When you forget who your Father really is and begin to doubt Him, the Holy Spirit will teach you again and remind you of His love, and gentleness, and kindness.

Further Reading: Matthew 10:19, Luke 11:13, 1 John 2:27

Your Father will tell you what no one else knows to help you believe Him.

Read: John 14:28-31

Jesus told His disciples on multiple occasions that He would be killed and resurrected on the third day. He told them many such bits of truth, which the Holy Spirit brought to their remembrance later. In John 14:29, He said the reason He told them beforehand was to help them believe. Even after personally walking with Jesus for three years, listening to Him teach, and witnessing all the miracles, He knew the disciples would doubt Him in crisis.

Has your Father ever told you something to help you believe? Maybe you've sat in a church service and wondered if the pastor read your diary because he was speaking directly to you. Maybe you received an anonymous donation of exactly the amount of money or other provision you were needing. Or maybe a friend or acquaintance sent you an encouraging note or a Bible verse that spoke to your broken heart after a tragedy. Sometimes the Holy Spirit will let someone know beforehand what is coming down the pike, but many times it isn't clear until after the fact that He was preparing you all along. If you are struggling to believe your Father, ask Him to reveal Himself to you in order to help you believe. He is delighted with your honesty and vulnerability.

Further Reading: Isaiah 46:9-10, Mark 9:24, John 1:50

Your Father believes you are worth it.

Read: John 15:1

Jesus compared the Father to a vinedresser – a gardener who takes care of a vineyard. Have you ever had a garden? It's a lot of work! Someone who takes care of a vineyard has to devote hours and hours of work to the plants. When he does, those plants produce lots of good fruit. Caring for a vineyard is a daily job. Constant attention to the vines – fertilizing, watering, pruning, supporting branches, and getting rid of pests – is a necessary part of the job.

Your Father believes you're worth His time and attention. He focuses on you every day, desiring to water and nourish you with His Word. He prunes dead and diseased branches, and He lifts up connected branches that are laying in the dirt. Your messes aren't too messy for Him. You aren't too needy for Him, and you are never an inconvenience. He delights in caring for you. Press in to the process today. Read His Word. Listen for His voice. Invite His pruning into your life. Entrust yourself to the perfect Gardener.

Further Reading: Psalm 8:3-5, Hebrews 12:2, Psalm 51:10

Your Father values relationship more than rule-keeping and task-doing.

Read: John 15:2-6

After the Last Supper, Jesus and His disciples walked past some vineyards on the way to the Garden of Gethsemane to pray. Jesus began giving them His last words of instruction as they walked. He compared Himself to the vines they saw, and the rest of us to the branches bearing the fruit. Jesus didn't give His disciples a to-do list before He went to the cross. He didn't give them three steps to reach the whole world. He told them to stay connected to Him.

The Father is more concerned about your connection to Him than He is about the fruit you bear. In fact, the original Greek word for "cuts off" in John 15:2 actually means "picks up" (same word used in John 5:8 and John 8:59). When you're laying in the dirt, not producing as much fruit as you could, your Father picks you up and supports you with the stronger branches connected to the Vine. We sometimes get overwhelmed because we're so focused on production, and our Father wants us to focus on connection. He yearns for relationship with you. He wants you around all the time! Revel in His longing for you today.

Further Reading: Psalm 139:1-18, 1 John 3:1

Your Father will shape your desires by His own as you abide in Him.

Read: John 15:7

As they walked toward the Garden of Gethsemane, passing a vineyard along the way, Jesus spoke to His disciples about abiding in Him. In John 14:7, the Greek word for "abide" also means "continue, dwell, endure, be present, and wait for expectantly." Jesus pointed out that abiding in Him is active and ongoing. He wanted His followers to continue meditating on what He'd said, keep their faith no matter the hardship, and wait expectantly for Him to act. Then, Jesus said, they could ask Him to fulfill their desires because they would match His.

Your Father longs to spend time with you. He wants to show you the best way to navigate your situation. He desires your priorities to line up with His because He knows that is what's best for you. The more time you spend with your Father and the more you meditate on who He is, the more your wishes will line up with His. What does it look like for you to abide in Your Father today?

Further Reading: Psalm 37:4, Psalm 145:14-19

Your Father gives you the choice to abide in Him and make your home with Him.

Read: John 15:8-11

What does it mean to abide in the Father's love? Think of it this way. A dog has a fence around the back yard where he lives, and as long as he stays there, he has plenty of food and fresh water and cuddles. However, if he chooses to run away, he loses the benefits of his owner's love for him. His owner won't love him less if he runs away, but he is no longer able to abide in his owner's love.

Your Father longs for you to abide in His love. He wants to lavish blessings on you, but you've got to stick with Him. He gives you the choice to turn your back on Him, but if you do, His broken heart drives Him to watch for your return day and night. Dear Child, if you could only comprehend how great is your Father's love for you! Choose to abide in Him, and He will make your joy full to overflowing!

Further Reading: Luke 15:11-24, 1 John 3:1, Revelation 3:20

Your Father talks to you and calls you Friend.

Read: John 15:12-15

It was not common for a rabbi in the first century to call his followers "Friends," yet this is what Jesus called His disciples. He said the test of their friendship was the same as the test for their love of Him: obedience. The gift that Jesus brought to the friendship was revelation. Jesus kept no secrets. He shared with His friends all that the Father told Him and literally manifested the Father to them in bodily form.

Your Father wants you to know what He's up to. He wants to share His eternal perspective with you, and He desires for you to join Him in the work He's doing around you. He loves using ordinary people – little children like you and me – to accomplish His mission. When you obey Him, He can achieve through you what you never thought possible.

Further Reading: Exodus 33:11, Proverbs 18:24, James 2:23

Your Father chose you!

Read: John 15:16-17

Jesus intentionally chose the disciples to follow Him, to learn from Him, to carry on His mission, and to experience the special love He had for them. He chose this intimate group of twelve men to learn how to love like Him. The custom of the day was for prospective students to ask a rabbi to allow them to follow and learn, but this was not the case for Jesus' followers. Jesus pursued each of them and invited them to follow and learn from Him.

You didn't seek a relationship with your Father before He pursued you. You didn't love Him before He loved you, nor did you make the decision to belong to Him before He drew you to Himself. Your Father had His eye on you when He was forming you in your mother's womb. He made you on purpose, and specifically designed you to fulfill your calling. You are wanted and loved. You are indispensable. Your Father chose you to be His child and show other people the way to Him. He chose when you would be made and where you would be born. All along, He's been weaving the threads of your story together with the threads of others' stories to make a beautiful tapestry. Enjoy being His chosen child today.

Further Reading: Jeremiah 1:5, Acts 17:26-28

Your Father knows what it's like to be hated.

Read: John 15:18-25

Jesus never did wrong to anyone. He never sinned at all. He was the embodiment of love because "God is Love" (1 John 4:16). His behavior and character was impeccable, and yet He was hated. The religious leaders had in their heads who and what they expected the Messiah to be, and Jesus didn't live up to their expectations. Furthermore, He called them out on the condition of their hearts when they wanted to keep living in pious self-righteousness. So they hated Him.

Have you ever been hated? Called names? Made fun of? Your Father knows what that feels like. Have you been ostracized? Rejected? Abused? Your Father understands. He endured ill treatment at the hands of evil men even though He was completely innocent. He loved them so much He chose to send His Son to die for them, and still they hated Him. Your Father sees you. He knows all that you have been through. He desires to help you forgive those who have hated you and hurt you. No matter what, you can know that you are the apple of your Father's eye. You have a Father who is constantly lavishing His love on you, even when others do not. Rest in His love today.

Further Reading: Psalm 25:15-21, Zechariah 2:8

Your Father has given you the greatest gift ever!

Read: John 15:26-27

Jesus told His disciples they would be hated and persecuted and even killed for following Him. Then He gave them words of comfort and encouragement. He didn't say, "It's going to be alright," or "It will all be worth it." He told them He would send them a Helper who would be just like Him. The Spirit of Truth, He said, would be His presence with them every single moment. The Holy Spirit would be their Comforter, Counselor, Confidante, and Friend – just like Jesus had been.

Your Father gives the Holy Spirit to everyone who puts their trust in Him. That means He sees every move you make and all the work you do. He is with you every moment to see how you are treated, what is happening in your life, what responsibilities you have. He understands you better than you understand yourself! Any time you feel alone or don't know what to do, He is there, and you can ask Him for help. When you get frustrated because nothing is going the way you think it should, ask Him to show you what He is up to. Your Father's presence with you every single moment changes everything!

Further Reading: Acts 2:38, Luke 11:11-13, Acts 1:8, John 14:26

Your Father will always prepare you for what's ahead.

Read: John 16:1-4

The words in John 14-17 are sometimes called Jesus' last discourse. His last words to the disciples prepared them to face not only the next few hours and days but also the rest of their lives. He strengthened them with encouragement and comfort. He told them what to expect and how to handle the hard times ahead. Jesus knew what His followers needed to hear in order for them to keep the faith in stormy seasons, and He provided for them perfectly.

Have you ever read a scripture or had a friend encourage you and then discovered it was just what you needed to endure a trial? Your Father knows when turbulence will come. He knows exactly what you need to persevere and hold tight to Him. He's so good to prepare you to hear His voice and follow Him through tough times. Maybe you've experienced hardships and feel like He wasn't there. Ask the Holy Spirit to show you the hand of your Father in the season of struggle. I promise you, He was there – preparing you, protecting you, pursuing you, and providing for you.

Further Reading: Psalm 139:5, Isaiah 43:2, Isaiah 45:2

Your Father knows the questions in your heart, even when you don't ask them.

Read: John 16:5-6

Jesus knew His disciples were wondering where He was going when He told them He was leaving. None of them asked the question, but Jesus already knew what was in their hearts. He knew they were filled with sorrow at the thought of Him not being with them anymore. They didn't have to say a word for Him to understand how they were feeling and what prompted those emotions. Jesus just knew.

Your Father knows the questions in your heart. He knows your doubts and sorrows. In fact, He understands why you feel the way you do even when you don't. He cares so much. He may not answer your questions the way you want Him to, but He will certainly speak to you about them. You must only listen. Take your heart and all that is in it to your Father today. Listen for His encouragement, His comfort, His reproof, His love. Dear One, He knows you better than you know yourself.

Further Reading: Mark 2:8, Psalm 139:4

Your Father is irresistible.

Read: John 16:6

When Jesus told His followers He would soon be leaving them, their hearts were filled with sorrow. No one wanted Him to leave! Do you remember how many times we've read in John's gospel that the crowds followed Jesus? People were drawn to Him. They wanted to be with Him. They longed to be touched by Him and hear Him teach. People just couldn't resist Jesus.

People are also captivated by the Father. You are being drawn to Him even now. He gives life and purpose and courage. When you really get to know Him, it's hard to resist Him. When you experience the joy of being in His presence, you won't want to leave. Spend time today meditating on what you love about your Father. Think about why you want to spend time with Him. Let Him show you how He is drawing you nearer to Himself.

Further Reading: Psalm 84:10, Matthew 14:13, John 6:68

Your Father does what is best for you, even if it hurts initially.

Read: John 16:7-11

Jesus encouraged the disciples by saying it would be good for Him to leave so He could send them the Holy Spirit. While Jesus walked this earth, He was bound by time and space. He couldn't be with each of them unless they were all in the same place. He knew it would be better for them to have the Holy Spirit – His constant presence with them and His words to each of them, perfect for every moment. He reminded them His plan was good, even if it didn't feel good right away.

Your Father has a good plan for you, too. He knows what doesn't feel good to you now, but He is more than able to bring good out of it. His plans really are best. He can be trusted because His love for you is so great. He is always acting out of love for you. Can you surrender to Him today, no matter what is going on in your life? Tell your Father how much you trust Him. If that's too hard, tell Him why you struggle to trust Him. He can handle it. Ask Him to show you His plan and comfort you with His great love.

Further Reading: Jeremiah 29:11-13, Romans 8:28

Your Father will only give you what He knows you can bear.

Read: John 16:12-15

Jesus had so many things to tell His friends in the hours before His death, but He didn't pile on them more than they could bear. Everything He told the disciples was out of concern for them. He knew the limits of what they could handle, and He lovingly told them so.

Your Father knows your limits, too. It may not seem like it at the moment, but He knows what you can and can't handle. Don't misunderstand. You weren't made to be self-sufficient, so He will probably give you more than you can handle *by yourself* at some point. He wants you to draw near to Him so He can help you navigate this life. In fact, He desires abundant life and overflowing joy for you, dear Child. Your Father will not heap up on you more than you can bear as you walk with Him. Draw close to Him today. He is for you.

Further Reading: 1 Corinthians 10:13, 2 Corinthians 12:9, James 4:8

Your Father will never let the hard times last forever.

Read: John 16:16-20

Jesus knew His disciples were about to face the hardest season of their lives. They were going to be confused as they watched Him die. Later, they would be persecuted and almost all of them martyred for their faith. Jesus reminded them that life would be very hard for a little while, but they would see Him again. I wonder if Jesus had His resurrection in mind when He said these words to His friends. Or maybe He was considering their eventual homecoming to Heaven after their hard work on earth was accomplished. Either way, the hard times would not last forever.

No matter how hard life is for you right now, your Father is still working. Your situation on earth may not change soon. Your season may last a lot longer than you had hoped, but never forget that the hope of Heaven is yours. You have so much to look forward to. Your Father is orchestrating the details of your life to bring you to a place of eternal bliss with Him. Hold on, Dear One. He still has plans to make everything better.

Further Reading: Psalm 18:19, Psalm 138:8, 1 Peter 1:6-9

Your Father specializes in turning grief into joy.

Read: John 16:20-22

Jesus told His friends to hold on because their grief would eventually be turned to joy. He didn't say the grief would leave and joy would come. He assured the disciples that the very object of their grief would become the object of their joy. He compared the pain they would soon endure to childbirth. When a mother survives natural labor and delivery, there comes a time when she thinks she won't make it. However, when it's all over, the baby in her arms that caused her so much pain brings her unspeakable delight. Jesus told His disciples to keep their eyes on the joy to come, so they would be able to persevere through the pain of His unjust trial and violent death, and the persecution they would have to endure.

Think about the worst pain in your life right now. Your Father specializes in turning what overwhelms you with grief into joy. No matter how difficult life is for you in this moment, Your Father understands why you are hurting, and He has plans to heal your broken heart. Believe it or not, He doesn't just stitch up your gaping wounds and heal them; He actually will bring good from them. That's His forte. It's what He does! He is always working for the good of those who love Him.

Further Reading: Genesis 50:20, Isaiah 61:1-3, Romans 8:28

Your Father speaks the way you need Him to.

Read: John 16:23-25

Jesus was a master teacher. He tailored the lessons to His audience. He knew what His disciples needed to hear from Him in order to understand. He knew how much they could handle, and what He needed to say to help them remember His words. There were times He spoke in figurative language, and there were times He spoke plainly. He often used small stories to illustrate His point. He usually connected what He was saying to commonplace situations the people already understood (i.e. agriculture, weather, animals). Jesus spoke in such a way that the ones who heard Him would get it.

Your Father knows what it will take for you to understand what He's trying to say to you. He knows what you need to experience to appreciate His character. He will speak to you in the way that is perfect for you. Your Father not only speaks especially to you; He orchestrates the details of your life so you can know Him personally. Be on the lookout for manifestations of His love for you: the beauty of His creation, the awesome sunset, a word of encouragement, or the peace He provides. Listen to what He is saying to you today.

Further Reading: Isaiah 28:23, Matthew 13:34, 1 Kings 18:20-39

Your Father gave up constant communion with His Son in Heaven for thirty-three years...to save *you* and make you His child.

Read: John 16:26-29

Jesus has always been with His Father (John 1:1). Even before time began and He created the earth, He always was. Until He came to earth, Jesus was never hungry or thirsty or sick. He had the whole earth and everything in it at His disposal. He wasn't limited by time or space or gravity. He knew the Father's rescue plan included sending Him to become the final sacrifice for our sins, but until that time, He dwelt in riches and power beyond our imagination.

Your Father believes you are worth all the pain and poverty His Son endured here on earth. Even if you were the only person alive on this planet, He still would have sent Jesus just for you. He loves you that much! Your Father was willing to endure injustice, rejection, and the most horrific death imaginable just so He could save you and make you His child. Dear One, you have always been worth it to Him. Ponder His great love and sacrifice for you today.

Further Reading: John 3:16-17, Hebrews 12:2-3, Zephaniah 3:17

Your Father already has victory over darkness, so you can have peace.

Read: John 16:30-33

Jesus was on His way to the Garden of Gethsemane, where He would be arrested and taken away to His death. He had already warned the disciples of the trials just around the corner, and now He encouraged them with the words, "In this world you will have trouble, but take heart. I have overcome the world" (John 16:33). He wouldn't have told them to take heart if they couldn't. Jesus already had victory over the darkness that would soon seem to be winning when our Savior was crucified.

Your Father is the reason Jesus said, "I have overcome the world." This world is a very hard place to live sometimes. As I write this devotion, there is racial tension and violence erupting in my city. The President sent in the National Guard yesterday to handle the riots. There seems to be unrest all over the place. Maybe you don't live in a dangerous place, but does the unrest in your heart threaten your security? Your Father offers you peace that does not depend on your circumstances. He wants to calm your soul and help you trust Him. No matter what is going on in your life, no one can take Your Father from you, or change His plans to spend eternity with you.

Further Reading: Psalm 18:16-19, Isaiah 26:3-4, 2 Corinthians 4:8-10

Your Father wants you to rely on Him to give you glory.

Read: John 17:1-3

Jesus prayed His final prayer in the Garden of Gethsemane as recorded in John 17. He started praying by asking His Father to give Him glory so He could glorify the Father. Jesus understood that the praise of man meant nothing unless He had the praise of His Father. He knew whose opinion mattered most, and He also knew He could turn people's eyes to the Father with the glory He received.

Your Father's thoughts about you are absolutely true. He gives you value and honor because you belong to Him, not because of anything you do or don't do. Your Father holds you in the highest esteem because you are His precious child. He wants His opinion to matter most to you. When you are honored by Him, you can let go of the pressure of pleasing the people around you. You don't have to live up to everyone else's expectations. Focus your attention today on Your Father's opinion, which matters most.

Further Reading: Psalm 22:25, Acts 5:29, James 4:6

Your Father gives His children specific work to do, and a special purpose.

Read: John 17:4-5

Jesus' words in John 17:4 give us a special insight into our Father's character. He likes work! He gave us the first example of work when He created the world and told Adam to take care of the Garden of Eden (Genesis 2:15). We were made to work. That said, work takes on many different forms, and we are not all called to the same work. The Father gave Jesus a special job to do. He intentionally gives us special jobs to do too.

Do you know you were deliberately designed? God formed you purposefully and masterfully in your mother's womb. He had good works in mind for you before you were ever born! It excites me to know my Father has created a specific place in this world for me, a special role for me that no one else on earth can fill. Maybe you feel like your life is meaningless or you're headed nowhere fast. Your Father desperately wants to show you the plans He's had for you from the beginning of time. Oh, how He delighted in creating you – the one and only you!

Further Reading: Jeremiah 1:5, Ephesians 2:10, John 14:12

Your Father has always desired to reveal Himself to you.

Read: John 17:6-8

One of the primary reasons the Father sent Jesus to earth was to reveal His character to us. Remember, Jesus was the "radiance of His glory and the exact representation of His nature" (Hebrews 1:3). The Father sacrificed what was most important to Him – Jesus – so you could *know* Him. The Greek word Jesus used for "come to know" in John 17:7 is *ginosko*. We've studied this word before. It means "to feel, understand, be resolved, or be sure." Jesus told the Father that His disciples had experienced Him and knew Him intimately.

Your Father understands that when you know Him – really *ginosko* Him – it changes everything. When you look to Him for identity, purpose, love, and fulfillment, you can resist the temptation to meet those needs with other people or habits. He made you to be in constant communion with Him. Only then will you experience the abundant life and fullness of joy that He had in mind when He made you. Dear One, knowing your Father is your highest calling.

Further Reading: Psalm 25:14, John 15:15

Your Father claims His children.

Read 17:9-10

Jesus spent time praying for His closest friends on the night He was arrested. He unashamedly called them His own. He claimed Peter with his rash impulsivity. He claimed Thomas, though He knew how he would doubt. He claimed James and John, who had pridefully argued over who was better. Jesus was not ashamed of His disciples' imperfections and struggles. Even knowing they would soon abandon and betray Him, He called them His own.

Your Father claims you as His child in spite of your flaws and your sins. He even uses your weakest moments to show how strong He is. He will not disown you in your struggles. He accepts you as you are, and He's pleased with you just because you are His child. If you have accepted Jesus, you belong to your Father, and that will never change.

Further Reading: Isaiah 43:1, 2 Corinthians 12:9

Your Father wants you to rest in His name.

Read: John 17:11-12

Jesus prayed to the Father, "Keep them in Your name." Or as another translation says, "protect them in the power of Your name." The Greek word He used for "keep" was *tereo*, which means "to guard, by keeping the eye upon, to preserve, to watch." Jesus was asking the Father to keep His eye on those He loved, to guard and protect them *in His name*. The Father's name represents His character – who He is. Jesus asked that the Father would act in accordance with who He is to unite His followers, protect them, strengthen them, and give them rest.

Your Father wants you to know His character. He wants you to experience Him as *Jehovah Rapha*, the God who Heals (Exodus 15:26). He is *El Shaddai*, God Almighty, the All Sufficient One (Genesis 17:1). He is *Jehoveh Jireh*, the Lord who will provide for you (Genesis 22:14). Your Father is *Jehovah Shalom*, your Peace (Judges 6:24). He is Holy (Isaiah 5:16), like no one else you have ever known before. You have a Father whose name and character can give you security, joy, and rest.

Further Reading: Proverbs 18:10, Matthew 11:28-30

Your Father keeps you out of the power of the evil one.

Read: John 17:13-16

Jesus prayed to the Father for protection for His disciples as long as they walked on this earth – and He knew how long that would be. For a time, this world is full of evil, but one day, Jesus will return to conquer once and for all (Revelation 6:2). In the meantime, He protects His own. The Father will not allow anything to happen that He cannot use for good. He promised (Romans 8:28). We may not understand the good on this side of Heaven because we can't see the big picture, but He can be trusted.

No matter what's going on in your life or what has happened to you in the past, consider that you really can't comprehend how your Father has protected you. Many times, we don't even realize when His hand has intervened for us. Furthermore, there are some things He keeps off limits to the enemy. Your Father won't allow anyone or anything else in life to endanger your identity or your eternity. He has made you His own, and nothing can change that.

Further Reading: Deuteronomy 1:31, Psalm 91:14-16, 2 Thessalonians 3:3

Your Father uses the truth to transform you.

Read: John 17:17-19

Contrary to popular opinion, Jesus not only claimed there is an absolute truth, but also that He *is* that absolute truth (John 14:6). Even secular psychology tells us that our actions are birthed of feelings, feelings are controlled by thoughts, and thoughts are dictated by beliefs. In other words, beliefs drive thoughts, which drive feelings, which drive behavior. Have you ever wondered why you do what you do? Every action can be traced to a belief in your heart. Are you sitting in a chair you believe will hold you up? Did you eat a meal recently because you believe your body needs food? Think about what beliefs drive your behavior.

Your Father desires to transform your thoughts and emotions and actions by leading you to believe what is true. Here are some truths you can hang on to for dear life: Your Father is good (Psalm 119:68). Your Father "celebrates and sings because of you, and He will refresh your life with His love" (Zephaniah 3:17, CEV). Your Father is faithful even if you are not (2 Timothy 2:13). Meditate on the truth of the Word today, and let your Father transform you.

Further Reading: John 8:32, Romans 12:2

Your Father had YOU on His heart two thousand years ago as He prepared to sacrifice His life for you.

Read: John 17:20-21

Jesus prayed for His disciples right before He was arrested, but He also prayed for you! Check out John 17:20, which says, "I do not ask on behalf of these alone, but for those also who will believe in Me through their word." You have believed because the disciples shared the gospel after Jesus ascended back into Heaven. Those who were saved then shared with others...who shared with others...who shared with others...who eventually shared the gospel with the person who led you to Jesus. So Jesus was praying for you!

Your Father was thinking of you when He formulated a rescue plan to spare you eternal separation from Him. I've said it before, and I'll say it again: If you were the only person on earth, He still would have sent Jesus to be the sacrifice for your sins. Oh dear Child, your Father loves you more than you can imagine! He is willing to go to any length to have you spend eternity with Him. Your Father acted to save you because He believes you are worth it.

Further Reading: Isaiah 53:3-11, Acts 2:23

Your Father has made you part of a very large family!

Read: John 17:22-26

Jesus prayed again and again for unity among believers. Since each of us is called a child of God, we are brothers and sisters. Jesus prayed that our family would be characterized by unity, love, and purpose. Our mission is to live together in such a way that those outside our family can see what it means to be a child of our Father.

Maybe you have been hurt or rejected by your natural family. Maybe they've abandoned you. Your Father wants you to know you belong in *this* family. You have siblings all over the world who love you and would even give their lives if it would allow you to know your Father better. In other words, you are not in this alone. Your Father knew you would need the support and love of a whole family to live this life on mission. So He gave us each other. Meet with some brothers or sisters this week and consider how your love and unity can show the world around you how wonderful your Father really is.

Further Reading: Galatians 6:10, Romans 11:17, Hebrews 10:25, 1 Peter 5:8-10

Your Father doesn't run away from hard things.

Read: John 18:1-5

Jesus knew all that was going to happen to Him after He was arrested. Instead of hiding in the garden where He had been praying, Jesus went out to meet the crowd of soldiers and religious leaders. He was going to face them head on because He knew that was part of His mission. He didn't pretend to be someone else when they told Him who they were looking for. He bravely surrendered Himself into their hands.

You will have hard circumstances in your life. You may be tempted to push them out of your mind and try to forget about them. You may want to run away and start a new life in a new state. You will probably want to avoid the subject and isolate yourself from other people, but this isn't the way to handle difficult situations. Your Father can give you the courage to face problems with Him, just as Jesus did. Press in to your Father with your tough stuff today. Ask Him what He is trying to accomplish as you face it together.

Further Reading: Psalm 42:11, James 5:16

Your Father has so much power in His voice, He doesn't need to use physical strength against the enemy.

Read: John 18:4-6

When the mob came to arrest Jesus, He asked them who they were seeking. "Jesus the Nazarene," was their answer, to which He responded with two powerful words: "I AM." The Jewish religious leaders who were in the angry crowd would have understood Jesus' claim to deity in that statement. In the Old Testament, when Moses asked God for His name, He said, "I AM" (Exodus 3:14). There was so much power in Jesus' voice that everyone drew back from Him and fell on the ground! It's important to understand that Jesus didn't have to go with the mob who was arresting Him. He was in complete control, but He *chose* to turn Himself over to them for your sake.

Can you imagine how much power is in the voice of your Father? I'm not talking about power that manifests in anger and volume and dominance, but power that can make your enemies fall flat on the ground. Power that can change the direst of circumstances. Power that can call into being what was never there before. Power that can heal the deepest wounds and soften the hardest heart. It was the powerful voice of your Father that created the entire universe. Let Him use that powerful voice today to speak life and peace into you as only He can.

Further Reading: Genesis 1:3, Romans 4:17, Psalm 51:10

Your Father is protective of His children.

Read John 18:7-9

Jesus had eleven of His closest friends with Him in the garden when the mob came to arrest Him, and even though His life was in danger, He was concerned for the safety of His own. He told the soldiers and religious leaders who came for Him, "…If you seek Me, let these go their way." Jesus was ready to lay down His life because He knew that was His mission. That was the rescue plan for all mankind, but it was not yet time for the disciples to face their end.

No matter what's going on around the world, no matter how many people are suffering or endangered, your Father has His eye on you. He's protective of you and ready to defend. He cares about even your smallest concern. You are constantly under His watch. He never stops guarding you and saving you. You won't know until you stand before your Father face to face how many times He protected you. Oh, how much He loves you!

Further Reading: Zechariah 2:8, Psalm 121:7, Isaiah 43:1-4, 2 Thessalonians 3:3

Your Father desires to heal those caught in the crossfire of sin.

Read: John 18:10-11 and Luke 22:50-51

Remember, Jesus is the perfect picture of the Father — your Father and mine (see John 10:30, 12:45). So Jesus was always acting on the emotion, direction, and desires of the Father. When Jesus was arrested, Peter had a moment of acting out in his anger and cut off the ear of the high priest's servant, Malchus. Did Jesus respond with, "Way to go, Peter! Be brave!" No. Jesus was concerned for the innocent one who had no choice but to follow his master into a dangerous situation. Malchus was blindsided by the sword heading his way. He was harmed by the sins of his master and people he had maybe never even met.

Your Father desires to heal your wounds, created by the sins of others. Have you been harmed by other people? We all have — some more than others. If your heart is heavy and struggling to forgive, know that your Father is on your side. He loves you more than you can imagine, and He desires to heal your wounds. He is defensive of you, and is willing to do anything you need to restore you. Enjoy the promise of His healing touch today.

Further study: Psalm 103:1-6, Romans 3:23, Matthew 4:23

Your Father allowed His Son to be bound and arrested...for you.

Read: John 18:12-14

Do you remember how the angry mob fell down when Jesus asserted His deity by calling Himself, "I AM?" He had all the power to save Himself, yet chose to be bound. He chose to follow the soldiers to trial. Isaiah prophesied that it would be this way. "Like a lamb that is led to slaughter, and like a sheep that is silent before its shearers, so He did not open His mouth" (Isaiah 53:7). He was bound and determined to fulfill His mission to save mankind from their sins – to save *you* from yours.

Your Father chose how He would sacrifice His Son. In His absolute holiness and justice, blood had to be shed for our sin. Someone had to be punished for all the wrongs we have done or will do. Otherwise, we could never be in our Father's presence. Jesus lived a perfect, sinless life, which made Him the perfect, sinless sacrifice to take the punishment for our sins so we never have to suffer eternally for them. Your Father loves you so much that He couldn't bear the thought of your separation from Him. He chose to be bound and arrested and tortured and killed so you can be together. Thank Him today for such great sacrifice.

Further Reading: Matthew 26:52-54, John 12:27

Your Father knows what it's like to be rejected and abandoned by a best friend.

Read: John 18:15-18, 25-27

Peter was one of Jesus' three best friends. He was part of the inner circle. He'd spent more time with Jesus during His ministry than perhaps any other person. He'd professed His unchanging devotion to Jesus and even sworn he would die for Him. Yet, when the pressure mounted, Peter denied that he even knew who Jesus was. Not once, not twice, but three times.

Have you been rejected and abandoned by someone you loved most? Your Father knows how that feels. You are not alone in your pain, and the burden of forgiveness is not yours alone. Your Father knows how hard it is to forgive such a personal attack – and yet He did. More than that, Your Father knows how difficult it is to forgive someone who's hurt His child, but He did. He will help you grieve the painful loss of relationship and also lead you every step of the way to forgiveness. He's walked the path before, and He knows best how to navigate it. Ask your Father to take your hand and show you the next step.

Further Reading: Psalm 55:12-23, Colossians 3:13

Your Father is humble and doesn't demand fair treatment.

Read: John 18:19-24

After Jesus was arrested, His accusers brought Him before the high priest to answer the charge of blasphemy (claiming to be God). He was unfairly doubted, accused, arrested, brought to trial, and abused. One of the officers with the high priest struck Jesus without cause. He had not been disrespectful. He merely spoke the truth, and for that He was reviled, yet Jesus never fought back. He never met might with might or fight with fight. He knew exactly who He was and what He came to do, so He didn't feel the need to defend Himself.

Your Father is confident in who He is, and all His actions are motivated by love, so He doesn't need to fight back when He's ridiculed. His contentment and self-assurance can give you security and peace. Even when people misjudge you or malign your character, you can know that your Father never will. He knows every single little detail about you, and He loves you anyway! In fact, He's crazy about you! Take your situation to Him today. Thank Him for His understanding, and rest in His love for you.

Further Reading: Isaiah 53:7, Philippians 2:5-8

Your Father knew what kind of death His Son would die, and He allowed it anyway.

Read: John 18:28-32

When Pilate, the Roman governor, questioned the Jewish leaders about Jesus' crimes, they didn't even give him an answer. In effect, they just said, "Why would we bring Him to you if He were not guilty?" The reason they brought Jesus to him in the first place was for a death sentence. The Jews were not permitted to put anyone to death without Roman law behind them. Jesus knew that's why He was standing before Pilate. He knew that grueling, tortuous, excruciating crucifixion was coming. And yet, He chose to follow through.

The writer of Hebrews tells us why Jesus continued to walk the road toward the cross when He could have killed all His enemies with a single word from His mouth. Hebrews 12:2 says He did it "for the joy set before Him." Beloved, *you* are the joy that was set before Him. He did it for you! The thought of saving you to spend eternity with Him was enough for your Father to sacrifice *everything*. You were enough motivation for Him to restrain the angels waiting to intervene, because *you* are worth it to your Father. Soak in that truth today. You, dear Child, are worth it!

Further Reading: Isaiah 53:10, 1 Peter 3:18

Your Father is wise with His words.

Read: John 18:33-37

When Jesus was questioned by Pilate, He told the truth. He didn't mince words or skirt the question. He could admit to no wrongs, because the accusations just weren't true, yet His answers were perfect to explain the situation He was in. Jesus knew how to speak the truth to every person He encountered. He knew what truth each one needed to hear. He was an expert at turning the leading questions of the religious people back on them. He was wise enough to evade their verbal traps and still never speak a lie.

It's comforting to have a Father who always has an answer. Even if you don't know what to say or how to explain, your Father can take care of that. He is never surprised by a question or accusation. He is always able to speak truth into your situation. He will always show you what to say through the Holy Spirit when you ask Him. You don't need to worry about your words or explanations. That hard conversation you are dreading…He has already gone before you. Your Father can handle it. Trust Him to speak truth to you – and through you – with just the right words.

Further Reading: John 1:17, John 16:13, Luke 12:11-12

Your Father has never done anything to make Him guilty.

Read: John 18:38-40

Pilate questioned Jesus again and again but found no guilt in Him. No surprise there! No one on earth could provide true accusations against Him because He never sinned. He wasn't like someone who looks good on the outside but is a different person behind closed doors. There are people who live a double life, but Jesus was never one of them. He always lived in the light. He was never ashamed of His own actions because He always did what the Father told Him to do.

If you are like me, you've believed that anyone who holds the title of "father" has to be guilty, but not your Heavenly Father. If someone has told you that He is holding out on you, it's not true. If you think He's abused you or abandoned you, that's not true either. If you believe your Father has ever acted toward you with any motivation other than love, that's a lie. He loves you more than life itself, and He proved it by enduring the worst death imaginable on your behalf. If you struggle to believe these truths, take your doubts to Him. Ask Him to show you His involvement in your life. He's always been there. Your Father has never done you wrong, and He never will.

Further Reading: 2 Corinthians 5:21, 1 Peter 2:22, 1 John 3:5

Your Father knows what physical and emotional pain feels like.

Read: John 19:1-5

Pilate thought the people would be satisfied with scourging Jesus for this blasphemy of which they accused Him. He was more concerned about what other people wanted than what was right. So he ordered our compassionate, healing, innocent Jesus to be whipped with thirty-nine lashes. It was believed that forty could kill a man, and no one was ready for that just yet. The soldiers used a leather whip with sharp pieces of bone and rocks tied into the cords that would catch human flesh and rip it from the back to expose the muscles and bones beneath. As if that wasn't enough, the soldiers mocked Jesus and bullied Him. They pushed a crown of thorns onto His head that caused blood to flow down His face until He was nearly unrecognizable.

Maybe you've been physically abused, or maybe you deal with chronic pain. Perhaps you've been bullied, mistreated, mocked, and made fun of. Your Father understands. You're not alone in your pain and anger. Your Father hurts for you and defends you, dear Child. One day, He'll make everything right because He is just and righteous. Take your hurts to Him. You can call Him *Abba*, as Jesus did, which is like calling Him *Daddy*. He longs to hold and comfort you today. When you are ready, fall into His embrace.

Further Reading: Isaiah 53:3-5, Psalm 22:24

Your Father is truthful, even when people hate Him for it.

Read: John 19:6-11

Many religions will acknowledge that Jesus was a real man who lived in the first century. They will call Him a good teacher or prophet, but refuse to admit He was both God Himself and the Son of God. If He was who He said He was (and that's the reason the Jews killed Him), then He didn't leave "good teacher" or "prophet" as an option for us. He was either a liar or a lunatic, or He really was Lord as He said. Even though people hated Him for speaking the truth and ultimately killed Him for it, Jesus never once told a lie.

Your Father loves the truth. Even when it's not popular, He wants you to know and understand the truth so you can respond to who He really is. That's why He continues to reveal Himself to you, little by little, so you will know Him. Some people are offended by the Father because He tells us the best way to live life – just like earthly parents tell their own children how to be safe and live a happy, fulfilling life. Trust me, He knows best. Your Father will always tell you the truth, and when you are listening, you are in a good place.

Further Reading: Psalm 25:5, Isaiah 45:19

Your Father is innocent.

Read: John 19:12-16

Jesus walked on this earth for thirty-three years and never sinned. Not once. If He had, He couldn't have been the perfect sacrifice to save us from our sins. The Jews accused Him of lying, starting riots, and leading people astray. Pilate, the Roman governor of the province, found Him "not guilty" on all accounts and charges. However, Pilate was afraid of the people. So he "washed his hands" to declare himself not responsible for an innocent man's death (Matthew 27:24) and handed Him over to be crucified.

You may disagree with your Father's will. You may even accuse Him of doing wrong, but here is the truth: Your Father is absolutely innocent. He *is* love (1 John 4:16), so He has never made a decision that was not based on His love for people. He never allows anything He cannot use for our good and His glory (Romans 8:28). Remember, you are your Father's child. He continues to love you even when you don't love Him. Precious Child, rest in the fact that your Father knows what He's doing, and He always does what is right.

Further Reading: Psalm 145:17, Daniel 4:37, 2 Corinthians 5:21, 1 Peter 2:22

Your Father submitted Himself to excruciating pain and public humiliation to pay the price for your sins.

Read: John 19:17-22

Jesus endured the torture of thirty-nine lashes that tore the skin from His back. He was silent when the soldiers mocked Him. He didn't resist when they stripped Him of His clothes and made Him carry the cross beam up a hill called Golgotha. The climax of His torture was when they nailed His hands and feet to the cross. Yet His heart was so full of love for the people who were abusing Him that He prayed, "Father, forgive them, for they don't know what they are doing" (Luke 23:34). Jesus' prayer for the forgiveness of His enemies extends to you across the centuries.

Your Father's heart was full of love for you on that day when Jesus was crucified. Your Father considered the cost. He weighed His options. Either He would be separated from you for eternity because He is holy and cannot be in the presence of sin, OR He would have to make Himself the perfect sacrifice once and for all so He could have you with Him for eternity. A wise man named Ugo Bassi once said, "Measure thy life by loss instead of gain…Love's strength standeth in Love's sacrifice." The strength of your Father's love is measured by the depth of His sacrifice. You, dear Child, are worth all He suffered. He would do it all over again to save you. He loves you that much.

Further Reading: Mark 10:45, John 15:13, Romans 5:6-8

Your Father gave prophecies about the Messiah in advance because He really wanted you to know Him.

Read: John 19:23-24

God prompted prophets of the Old Testament to write down predictions about the Messiah hundreds of years before Jesus was even born. They wrote down where He would be born (Micah 5:2), that He would be born of a virgin (Isaiah 7:14), and that He would spend a season of His life in Egypt (Hosea 11:1). They even prophesied that when He was betrayed to His death, the thirty pieces of silver paid to His betrayer would be used to buy a potter's field (Zechariah 11:12-13). Psalm 22:18 tells that His clothes would be gambled away when He was crucified. Over three hundred prophecies were written about the Messiah before He came to earth, and Jesus fulfilled every single one of them.

Your Father has always made a point of telling His children His ultimate plan. He has always made it a high priority to show His own how much He loves them. That's why He is revealing Himself to you now and teaching you personally who He really is. It is no accident that you're sitting here reading this book. Your Father is pursuing you and intentionally speaking to you. Oh, how He loves you!

Further Reading: Psalm 2:7 and Matthew 3:16-17, Psalm 8:2 and Matthew 21:16, Isaiah 50:6 and Matthew 26:67

Your Father knows what it's like to watch loved ones suffer.

Read: John 19:25-27

When Jesus was on the cross, He watched His mother and friends grieving. They experienced excruciating pain watching One they loved hurt so much. Not only were they losing Jesus, but it's implied they'd lost a loved one before. Jesus asked John to take care of His mother when He was gone. According to custom, when a woman was widowed, she entered the care of her eldest son, and if he was unable to care for her, he made other arrangements. Even in His most difficult hour, Jesus was concerned for the welfare of His mother, Mary, who it appears had already lost her husband.

Have you lost a loved one who you thought was your world? Maybe someone has hurt the one you love most? Your Father knows what it's like to hurt that badly. He knows what it's like to grieve with His closest friends and family. If you are grieving, He's grieving with you. He is moved by your pain because He loves you so much. Take your hurts to Him. He hurts with you and promises to hold you extra close. Enjoy your Father's comforting embrace today.

Further Reading: Psalm 34:18, Psalm 43:5, John 11:35

Your Father fought a battle for you and ended it with a victory cry.

Read: John 19:28-30

Jesus hung on the cross for six long hours before He died. After receiving some sour wine (fulfilling the prophecy in Psalm 69:21), He said the word, "*Tetelestai.*" This was the cry of a victor returning home from battle. This exclamation could also be translated, "Paid in full." Jesus' death on the cross was His final act of obedience that secured our future as children of God. Our sin debt was officially paid in full, and the battle to free our souls was won.

Your Father had the moment of Jesus' death on His mind from the beginning of time. It was so important to Him to spend eternity with you that He fought a hard battle, endured excruciating pain, and died a criminal's death. Your Father had a rescue plan in mind from the beginning of time so He could save you. You mean that much to Him.

Further Reading: John 3:16-17, 2 Peter 3:9

Your Father went out of His way to give you eye-witness accounts so you would believe Him.

Read: John 19:31-37

In the last two thousand years, people have tried to come up with every excuse to explain away the truth about our Savior. The Father foresaw many of those objections and answered them in advance. He knew people would doubt that Jesus really died, so He made sure it was recorded in scripture that blood and water flowed from where the spear pierced Jesus' side – medical proof that His heart had stopped. He made sure many people witnessed the death and burial of Jesus so they could all testify to the events that took place. Jesus fulfilled prophecies in His death that He could not have had control over (John19:36-37). Again and again, Jesus' identity and authenticity were proved to us so we would believe.

Do you know what your Father's highest priority is? He wants more than anything else for you to believe Him. He's been working for thousands of years to bring you to the point of trusting Him. Have you told Him you trust Him? Maybe today is the day you decide you trust your Father enough to receive His gift of salvation and eternity in Heaven with Him. Spend some time in prayer today, telling your Father what's on your mind. He can't wait to talk with you.

Further Reading: Acts 4:19-20, 1 John 1:1-3

Your Father knows what it's like for people to be ashamed of Him.

Read: John 19:38-42

Two men took Jesus' body down from the cross. It's interesting to note that both had been secret followers of Jesus because of their fear of losing status with the Jewish religious leaders. Neither Nicodemus nor Joseph of Arimathea wanted to be associated with Jesus during His life, but both sacrificed for Him in His death. Joseph provided a final resting place for Jesus' body, and Nicodemus gave enough spices for a royal burial.

Your Father knows not everyone will approve of your decision to follow Jesus. He knows that you may be criticized and ostracized for your choice to identify yourself as His child. Your Father knows what it feels like when people are embarrassed to be identified with Him. Just remember, it's His approval your heart desires most. Take your hurts and rejection to your Father. He will help you forgive and love the people who are ashamed of you, just as Jesus did.

Further Reading: Matthew 5:10-12, 1 Peter 3:14-17

Your Father can handle all the details.

Read: John 20:1-7

When Mary Magdalene and a few of her friends came to the tomb of Jesus that first Easter morning, they had no idea how they would move the stone to anoint His body with more spices (Mark 16:1-3), and yet they came. When they arrived, the stone had already been rolled away from the entrance of the tomb, and the burial face cloth was folded neatly. When Jesus was resurrected from the dead, the Father intentionally handled even the smallest details.

What circumstances in your life require meticulous attention to the details? Are there issues you don't have a clue how to handle? You don't have to carry the weight of the world on your shoulders, trying to make sure everything falls into place just so. That's not your responsibility. Your Father can handle it. Pray. Ask Him to intervene and take care of what you can't. He is more than capable. Trust Him to handle the details.

Further Reading: Matthew 17:27, Luke 9:13-17, Luke 22:10-13

Your Father gives understanding in His own perfect time.

Read: John 20:3-10

When John and Peter ran to the tomb that first Easter morning, they still didn't understand what the empty tomb meant. According to their own grasp of the prophecies, the Messiah surely would not be crucified! Jesus had explained a lot to them as they lived life together the past three years, but He wasn't ready for full disclosure until after the resurrection.

Surely there are situations in life that you don't understand. You have many questions for your Father – even unmet expectations of Him. You may not see the big picture until you stand with Him in Heaven, but one day, rest assured you will understand. He has promised to use all things for our good and for His glory (Romans 8:28), whether we see the fulfillment of that promise on earth or not. You can have confidence that your Father's timing is perfect.

Further Reading: Luke 24:26-32, Galatians 4:4-7

Your Father is tender, caring, and compassionate.

Read: John 20:10-18

Mary stood in the garden by the empty tomb after the disciples went home. She thought someone must have taken Jesus' body away, and she was grief-stricken. She stood there and wept, crying so hard that her tears blinded her to Jesus when He came and stood next to her. It wasn't until He said her name, "Mary," that she recognized her Lord. He only said one word to her, but it was the most important word He could have said. With that one word, Jesus poured out compassion on Mary and tenderly reminded her how much He loved her. He called her by name because He knew her and cared for her deeply.

Grief has a way of blinding us to the truth. We tend to judge our Father based on our circumstances instead of judging our situation through the lens of who our Father is. In the middle of your grief, your Father comes to you and calls you by name, Dear One. Remember, He's moved by your emotions. He sees you and tenderly reminds you how much He loves you. His voice is not harsh. If you listen closely, He will fill you with hope. Take your grief and disappointment to your Father today, and listen to Him call your name.

Further Reading: Psalm 63:1-8, Psalm 103:8-14

Your Father chooses people the world would not.

Read: John 20:18

The first person to whom Jesus revealed Himself after the resurrection was Mary Magdalene. She was the very first one Jesus entrusted with the responsibility of telling everyone that He had come back to life. In that day and age, women didn't have status as men did. Women couldn't even testify in a court of law. If someone had fabricated the story of the resurrection, they wouldn't have chosen a woman to be the first witness to spread the word. Furthermore, Mary had been demon-possessed (Luke 8:2), but her past did not disqualify her to be used by God.

You may feel *less than* or *second rate*, but you are *chosen* by your Father. Did you know there's no one in the entire world with your emotions and experience, no one else like you who could take your place you if you were gone? Not a single other person could fulfill the plan your Father has chosen for you. You are irreplaceable. Your value surpasses what you could even imagine. Out of everyone in the world, your Father chose *you* to live in the time and place you do. You are so special!

Further Reading: Ephesians 1:3-6, 2 Thessalonians 2:13-14

Your Father understands your mistrust and is ready to prove Himself to you.

Read: John 20:19-20

I love that Jesus' first words to His followers after the resurrection were, "Peace be with you." Don't we all crave peace? Take a deep breath and breathe in the peace your Father offers right now. After Jesus spoke peace to His friends, He showed them His hands and side. He didn't say to them, "Boys! I've been telling you for months now that I would die and come back to life! Why haven't you believed Me?" No. He understood the trauma they'd endured in witnessing His arrest, torture, and crucifixion. He knew why they doubted, and He stood ready to increase their faith.

Your Father knows all your life experiences. He knows why you don't trust Him as a Father – even if *you* don't know why. He wants to help you grow in your faith. He's ready to prove Himself to you, Dear Child, so you can trust Him more. I used to live in a cycle of doubt and fear, which led to disobedience, distance from my Father, and more doubt and fear. Now, I experience a new cycle: I trust my Father just a little, which leads me to obey. Then He shows me His faithfulness, which increases my trust in Him, so then I can obey a little more. He always proves Himself faithful to me. Ask your Father to reveal Himself to you and increase your trust in Him. He is always ready to do that.

Further Reading: Malachi 3:10, 2 Timothy 1:12

Your Father gives you discernment and authority as His child.

Read: John 20:21-23

When Jesus appeared to His disciples and proved that it was really Him, He breathed His Spirit on them. He gave them discernment and authority to speak the truth as the Holy Spirit spoke it to them. He didn't mean that they were authorized to declare who could be forgiven. He was giving them instructions to *announce* forgiveness to those who believed in Jesus as the atoning sacrifice for their sins and to preach warnings of guilt to those who refused to believe.

Your Father is drawing you close to Himself, not just for you, but for any who would believe as you share the truth with them. He wants you to build relationships with the people around you so they can know Him, too. What more loving thing could you do for someone than share the gospel with them? What would be better for them than receiving forgiveness for sins and becoming a child of God? Remember, He gave you His Holy Spirit to lead you when you first believed Him. Ask your Father if there is someone in your life with whom He wants you to share this journey.

Further Reading: Matthew 28:18-20, 2 Corinthians 1:3-4

Your Father knows and cares about what happens behind locked doors.

Read: John 20:24-29

Eight days after Jesus' resurrection, the disciples were gathered again in a locked room, and this time Thomas was with them. Jesus saw Thomas behind that locked door with a heart full of doubt and despair. He cared so much for Thomas that He went right through those locked doors to reveal Himself. The other disciples had seen Jesus already, so He walked straight up to Thomas and told him, "Reach here with your finger, and see My hands; and reach here your hand and put it into My side..."

Maybe you have some secrets about things that have happened behind closed doors. Maybe you, like Thomas, have built walls around your heart to protect you from getting hurt again. There's no hiding from your Father. He knows what happened, and He waits with open arms. He is not ashamed of you, but secrecy breeds shame. Ask Him for forgiveness if you had any choice in the matter. Ask Him to help you forgive anyone else involved. Ask your Father for a friend you can trust so you don't have to carry your secrets alone anymore. Your Father is delighted to heal the deepest, darkest parts of your heart. Oh Child, how He loves you!

Further Reading: Psalm 139:7-12, Luke 9:47, James 5:16

Your Father knows believing Him will always lead to blessing.

Read: John 20:29-31

Jesus didn't chide Thomas for his doubt, but He did pronounce a special blessing on all who believe *without* seeing Him. How could people know of Jesus and believe if they never saw Him? John answered that question himself: "These things are written that you may believe...and that by believing you may have life in His name" (John 20:31). The Holy Spirit prompted not just John, but all the people who wrote the scriptures so we could seek and know and believe Him.

Your Father has always desired for His children the blessings and abundant life that result from trusting Him. However, we must acknowledge that believing in Jesus causes suffering on this earth for many people. Can our Father really bless us when life feels so tragic and terrible? Yes! When we believe Him, His presence comforts us, His words encourage us, and His peace and joy fill our hearts. Furthermore, the apostle Paul tells us in Romans 8 that the blessings to come far outweigh our temporal suffering. Talk to your Father today, and ask Him to speak truth into the recesses of your heart where there is any unbelief. Take note of the blessings you have experienced already as a result of believing your Father. Let His faithfulness lead you to trust Him more.

Further Reading: Psalm 40:1-4, Jeremiah 17:7-8, Romans 8:16-18

Your Father sometimes lets you get desperate so you'll listen to Him.

Read: John 21:1-3

Whether Peter and the others were right or wrong in returning to their former occupation, the scripture doesn't say. Either way, they needed sustenance, and fishing was what they knew. So they went fishing. They fished all night long and didn't catch a single fish. If they had caught enough during the night, would they have listened to a "stranger" on the shore when He told them to do it differently? Probably not. Sometimes desperation drives people to listen to advice and try something else.

Your Father knows we're stubborn creatures, and sometimes desperation is the only thing that will push us in His direction. Remember, Jesus said, "Blessed are the poor in spirit, for theirs is the kingdom of heaven" (Matthew 5:3). He was pointing out a special blessing that comes with desperation. If you had all the companionship in life that you wanted, would you ever know your Father as a wonderful companion? If you never needed healing, would you ever get to know Him as your Healer? What if the most difficult circumstances – the ones that have made you most desperate – are the ones that drive you into the arms of your Father? What is it that makes you desperate for Him?

Further Reading: Psalm 107:12-13, Jeremiah 10:18, Isaiah 19:22

Your Father isn't always recognizable right away.

Read: John 21:3-4

Peter, together with six of the other disciples, decided to go fishing. They knew Jesus had risen from the dead, but they didn't know where He was or what He was up to that particular morning. They had fished all night long and caught nothing. They were no doubt frustrated, disappointed, and ready to give up. Then Jesus appeared on the shore, but they could not recognize Him. It took a miracle for them to see that it was the Lord.

In the same way, it's not always easy to identify what Your Father is doing. Were there periods in your life that make you wonder where He was? That has certainly been my experience. Then there came a day when I was told I could pray and ask the Holy Spirit to show me what my Father was doing in those seasons when I felt forgotten. Remember, your Father means for you to *never* be alone. He loves you too much to abandon you. So He was there. He was working. Ask Him to show you His hand in your life. He may not give you every answer you desire, but He wants you to know He was always protecting you, leading you, and comforting you – even if you didn't know it. He is for you, dear Child. He will never leave you nor forsake you (Deuteronomy 31:6).

Further Reading: Psalm 18:16-19, Isaiah 43:4

Your Father's kindness makes you able to run to Him after you've failed Him.

Read: John 21:4-7

After fishing all night and catching nothing, the disciples saw a man on the beach who told them to cast their nets on the other side of the boat. They probably wouldn't have listened except they were desperate. The location of the net probably wouldn't make a difference, but why not? They had nothing to lose. When a miraculously huge catch of fish started pulling on the net, John announced, "It is the Lord!" Peter couldn't wait to see, so he jumped into the sea to swim. Recall that Peter is the one who denied three times in Jesus' darkest hour that he even knew Him. And yet, he had experienced forgiveness so deeply that He didn't shrink away from Jesus. He didn't even hesitate for a moment.

Have you experienced your Father's forgiveness enough that you can run to Him? Do you still fear His wrath and judgment, or can you see His arms open wide waiting for you to come home to Him? Does your shame cause you to hide your face from Him? Maybe you need to ask Him to help you forgive yourself. Ask Him to help you see yourself as He sees you. Dear One, you are precious to Him, no matter what you've done. His mercy is abundant. His grace is no less than astounding. Oh, He is so kind and wonderful. Run to your Father today. Don't hesitate or shrink away. He is waiting with arms open wide.

Further Reading: Psalm 51:17, Romans 2:4, 1 John 1:9, 1 John 2:28

Your Father often provides for you before you even know you have a need.

Read: John 21:7-11

After Peter threw Himself into the sea to get to Jesus as fast as He could, the other six disciples brought in their miraculous catch of 153 fish. Yet, when they got to the shore, they found Jesus had already started cooking breakfast for them on a charcoal fire. Their stomachs were empty, and Jesus had made provisions to remedy that situation before they asked. He even helped the disciples acknowledge His provision when He told them to bring some of the fish they had just caught.

Dear Child, your Father knows everything you need. He's never surprised or caught off guard when you are. He knew before you did that you would require His provision, and He's delighted to take care of you. In fact, you will never know all the times your Father provided for you, protected you from unknown danger, or intervened in your life. His hand often goes unnoticed, but it's no less real and powerful. Beloved, if you struggle to see how He's provided for you thus far, ask Him to open your eyes. If you have seemingly insurmountable needs right now, take those to Him. Ask for His help. He may have already provided your answer.

Further Reading: Matthew 6:8, Isaiah 41:10, Matthew 6:25-34

Your Father is generous.

Read: John 21:12-14

Have you ever met someone who is so generous, they would literally give you the coat they were wearing? Jesus was that kind of person. Even though the disciples brought in a catch of 153 fish, they ate Jesus' fish and bread first. Jesus was happy to share with them. He delighted in His followers and enjoyed providing for their needs – even needs they didn't know about! Although He owned very little on this earth, Jesus was generous with all He had.

Your Father openhandedly provides for your needs, and even shares what is nonessential. Think about this: God could have made the world in black and white, but He made it in color. He could have made our bodies to use food only as fuel, but He gave us taste buds to enjoy our meals. He gave us so many marvelous things in nature to appreciate. Your Father loves to see you adore what He's made for you. Take a walk today, and spend some time thanking Him for His generosity and provision.

Further Reading: Psalm 37:23-26, Psalm 81:10, Matthew 20:1-15

Your Father invites you to love Him with your best, flawed love.

Read: John 21:15-17

Jesus met with Peter individually on the day of His resurrection (Luke 24:34, 1 Corinthians 15:5) and no doubt offered him forgiveness for his denials. Nevertheless, it was important for Jesus to publicly restore Peter. To do this, Jesus asked Peter to compare his love with that of the other disciples. Before Jesus' arrest Peter had claimed to love Him more than everyone else loved Him (Matthew 26:33). Jesus wanted Peter to examine his prideful view of his own love. Maybe this is why, when Jesus asked the question, "Do you love me?" the first two times, He used the Greek word *agapagas*, which means unconditional love. Peter answered twice with the Greek word *philio,* which speaks of more brotherly, reciprocal love. Maybe Peter was admitting that He loved Jesus with the best form of love his sinful, human heart could manage.

Your Father knows you have limitations to your love for Him. He understands how your sin nature causes you to struggle. Jesus asked Peter a third time, "Do you love Me?" – three times asked for three times denied. But the third time, Jesus used the word *philio*. He was saying to Peter, "Come to Me. Bring Me your imperfect love. It is enough." Your Father wants you to come to Him honestly. Bring your love for Him, whatever that looks like. He is holding out His hand, and will meet you where you are.

Further Reading: Deuteronomy 6:5, 2 Timothy 2:13, Ephesians 2:4-5

Your Father can be glorified by the death of His children.

Read: John 21:18-19

Jesus foreshadowed for Peter what sort of death he would die because of his devotion to spreading the gospel. John specifically points out that God would be glorified by Peter's martyrdom, and indeed He was. Ancient writers of extrabiblical sources tell us that Peter was eventually crucified with his head downwards, because he didn't consider himself worthy to be crucified in the same way as his Lord. Peter's willingness and patience in death furthered the cause of the gospel and glorified God.

Do you trust that your Father can be glorified, even by the most awful circumstances in your life? It's true. He promises to work all things together for good (Romans 8:28). Trust me; He's more than able to make the source of your grief become your greatest source of joy. Glorifying your Father will always lead you to joy as you listen to the Holy Spirit speak truth to you. He can use even the most difficult circumstances to point people in His direction. Dear Child, no matter what's going on in your life, ask your Father to show you how He is working for good in it. He's amazing like that!

Further Reading: Romans 8:28-39, 1 Peter 5:10-11

Your Father doesn't want you comparing yourself to others.

Read: John 21:20-23

When Jesus told Peter of the death by which he would glorify God, Peter asked Him, "What about John?" Jesus' answer is amazingly practical for all of us. He said, "...What is that to you? YOU follow Me!" Jesus knew of Peter's tendency to compare himself to others around him. He knew comparison would distract Peter from the mission. I'm convinced Peter never forgot that conversation. I'm sure the Holy Spirit brought it back to him every time he was tempted to compare himself to others.

Comparison is the enemy of contentment. It also has the power to extinguish your joy. Your Father has a very specific plan in mind for you, one that no one else on earth can fulfill. Focusing your attention on just who your Father calls you to be each day removes an enormous amount of weight from your shoulders. You only need to do what He asks of you. Don't aspire to be just like anyone else. What are the triggers that tempt you to make comparisons? Maybe taking a break from social media or a particular magazine is in order. I promise our Father's plans for you are far better than you could ever dream for yourself.

Further Reading: Psalm 25:4-5, Proverbs 16:9, Hebrews 12:1-2

Your Father wants you to know Him!

Read: John 21:24-25

John ends his gospel by reminding us that while everything he told us is true, he only gave us the highlights. No one could possibly write down everything Jesus said and did because the world couldn't hold that many books! Don't you love that ending to John's account? The whole gospel can be summed up in the following way:

Your Father doesn't want your relationship to be distant or strained or full of striving. He wants you to know who He really is so you can trust Him. Let me encourage you with this, Child: No matter who you have believed your Father to be, that doesn't change who He is. Read that one more time. No matter who you have believed your Father to be, that doesn't change who He is. He has always loved you unconditionally. He has always been faithful to you. He has always been kind and trustworthy and sovereign. Take some time today to declare these truths out loud. What better way is there to end this journey through John's gospel than to spend some time with your Father, sharing your heart? Dear One, He longs to be known and trusted by you. He loves you more than you can imagine!

Further Reading: 2 Timothy 1:9-10, Hebrews 10:22-23, 1 Peter 1:18-21

Reading Recommendations from the Author:

Father God: Daring to Draw Near by Dave Patty

The Jesus Storybook Bible by Sally Lloyd-Jones

In the Grip of Grace by Max Lucado

Music Recommendations from the Author:

I am Loved by Mack Brock

Good, Good Father by Chris Tomlin

In the Father's House by Cory Asbury

Room at the Table by Carrie Newcomer

Redeemed by Big Daddy Weave